Midi-Pyrénées

Work realised with the support
of the Conseil Régional de Midi-Pyrénées

Photoengraving: Graphocoop 47, 47510 Foulayronnes
Printing: Imprimerie Fournié, Fonsegrives, Toulouse
Graphic design: Bruno Douin
Layout and adaptation for English version: ACCORD, Toulouse

Midi-Pyrénées

REGION OF PASSIONS

MILAN

The spirit of the South

Midi-Pyrénées, this veritable crossroads of nations, has been open to a huge diversity of influences blowing in from all four corners of the earth since ancient times. Celts, Romans, Visigoths, Francs and Arabs have all left indelible traces in the form of physical remains or toponymic vestiges. More recently, Italians and Spaniards, Algerians, north Africans and northern Europeans have added their strata to the cultural palimpsest. These successive waves could so easily have fashioned a land with no soul, a jumble of differing peoples. In fact this melting pot of different races has spawned the most flamboyant of cultures, a civilisation which extends refinement to all areas of life, even its most everyday pursuits: gastronomy, singing, music, sport, leisure activities … Midi-Pyrénées is much more than a land or a language, it is the happiness of existing in this unique light, at once gentle and vibrant, maternal and voluptuous. All the rest – the beauty of its brick and stonework, the variety of its landscapes, the dynamism of a city at the vanguard of new technologies – all this is secondary, serving only to emphasise the primary, fundamental feature which has exerted its fatal attraction on all who came as conquerors: the Occitanian *douceur de vivre*, meridional sister to Du Bellay's *douceur angevine*.

What a paradox, that this gentle art of living should be born and nurtured in a region where violence informs both landscape – with vertiginous peaks, arid *causses* and mighty rivers – and people, whose passions are known to run high. But then, isn't the function of any civilisation to transform mankind's natural violence into an affirmation of life and the joy of being in this world, in other words to lend this violence form? Popular wisdom has it that "happy peoples have no history". Midi-Pyrénées is a perfect example of the contrary: if any population could be said to have achieved contentment despite a chequered history, it is this people of the south-west who, as Stendhal said of the Italians, have a gift for happiness, despite a past peppered with acts of derring-do and *coups de théâtre*, not least of which is the dramatic episode of the Albigensian crusade.

Certain commentators have looked on the latter as a kind of French War of Secession, proof at any rate that Occitania had been colonised by the Francs. And yet, less than two centuries later, in the famous dispute between Armagnacs and Burgundians, this same Midi was one of the few provinces to remain faithful to the Dauphin de Bourges, at a time when the whole of northern France, occupied by the English, had abandoned him. In more recent times, politicians originating from Occitanian lands – from Gambetta to Jaurès – have often been the brightest stars in the firmaments of the various republics. Midi-Pyrénées has played as great a part in the construction of France as other regions reputedly less recalcitrant, but has done so on its own terms: rebellious when all was plain sailing, faithful when the seas got rough… Politicians, artists, warriors, intellectuals, workers and peasants together illustrate the spirit of the south that Nietzsche extolled when talking of the music of Mozart: a certain alliance of ruse and fire, calculation and passion, great art and spontaneity.

This spirit can be found in all the landscapes and peoples of Midi-Pyrénées. It is the selfsame spirit which caused the towers of Saint-Sernin and the monastery of les Jacobins to be raised in the Middle Ages and which today inspires the engineers of Ariane or Airbus: the desire to pull free of the glebe and embrace the azure, although never quite forgetting the alluvium soil of man's origins. Possibly the secret of this land lies here, in its aspiration to a verticality which tempers the memory of its roots...

Midway between the Atlantic and the Mediterranean, with nearby Spain "pushing with its horn" (Claude Nougaro), Midi-Pyrénées, which returned to embrace the Orient and its dreams of light three centuries ago when the Canal du Midi was dug, can lay claim to the proud title of "middle of the world". It must now grasp the historic opportunity offered by the constitution of the European Union, whilst preserving its own particular charm: a certain quality of life not incompatible with economic dynamism. Indeed it is these two features that seduce the many northern Europeans coming to settle in the Occitanian sun belt, these qualities that may one day earn Toulouse the status of Eurocity, like Milan or Barcelona. For it is no longer enough, in order to seduce people, to speak the language of economic necessity, one must also use the words of the poet and celebrate the splendours of twilight over the Garonne, of red brick facades burning in the sunlight, and the perfume of a Cahors wine uncorked under the bower of Occitanian autumns…

Preface

Pierre Le Coz
Writer

The rocky peak of Montségur (Ariège)

Saint-Étienne cathedral square in Toulouse (Haute-Garonne)

A view of the Pyrenean chain (Hautes-Pyrénées)

Rooftops in Najac (Aveyron)

The river Lot at Saint-Cirq-Lapopie (Lot)

The banks of the Tarn and the cathedral of Sainte-Cécile in Albi (Tarn)

The Gers countryside near to Marciac (Gers)

The *bastide* of Auvillar (Tarn-et-Garonne).

Paths

of history

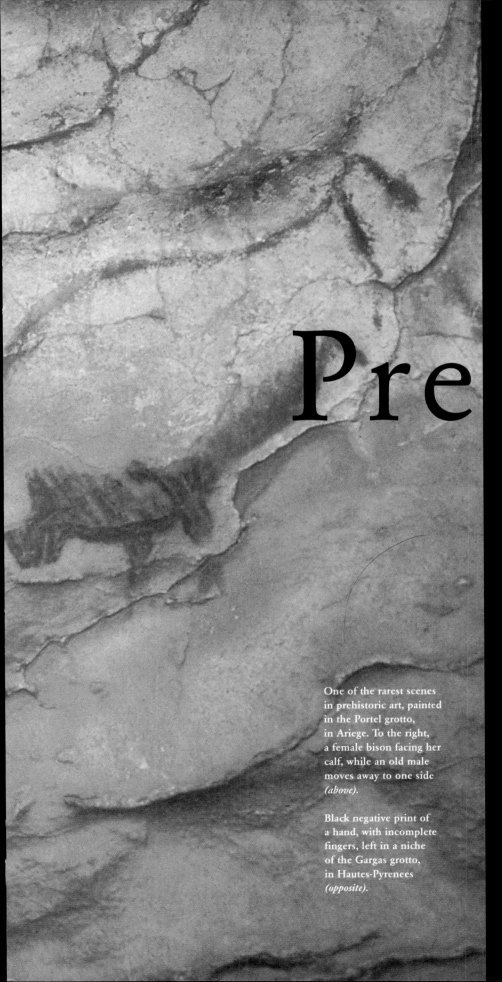

One of the rarest scenes
in prehistoric art, painted
in the Portel grotto,
in Ariege. To the right,
a female bison facing her
calf, while an old male
moves away to one side
(above).

Black negative print of
a hand, with incomplete
fingers, left in a niche
of the Gargas grotto,
in Hautes-Pyrenees
(opposite).

The cradle of civilisation

Jean Clottes & Jean Vaquer
*Palaeontologist and specialist of the
Neolithic Age*

Prehistory

FROM THE REMOTEST TO THE MOST RECENT, the prehistoric
peoples are richly represented in Midi-Pyrénées, which
has some of France's richest and most diversified remains,
with such famed sites as Niaux, Le Mas d'Azil and Trois Frères
in Ariège, Gargas in Hautes-Pyrénées, Gourdan in Haute-
Garonne, Pech-Merle and Cougnac in Lot, which are known
the world over.

Humankind was already living in our region at least one
million years ago. At Naterie,
in Gers, carved pebbles attributed to Homo Erectus have
been uncovered in contemporary layers of the Mindel
glaciation, between 850 000
and 600 000 B.C. On the
banks of the Garonne, a whole
range of tools made from
quartz and quartzite pebbles
have been found in the alluvial plains; they have been
dated from the Acheulean age.

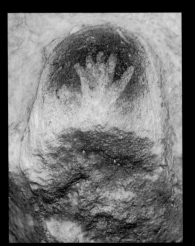

(Ariège). The open-air site at Mauran (Haute-Garonne) has revealed that the Mousterians there hunted bison in autumn. We know from the site at La Borde (Lot) that those living there preferred the aurochs. The climate was cold and dry: the last glaciation of the Würms age lasted, with climactic variations, right up to 10 000 B.C.

The last phase of the glaciation age, which began in 35 000 B.C., was marked by a succession of brilliant cultures: the Aurignacians, Gravettians, Solutrians and Magdalenians produced the cave paintings as well as ornate objects. Those hunter-gatherers, who lived in parties twenty or thirty strong, often spent several months in one area, as at Gourdan (Haute-Garonne), to get as much as they could out of the local habitat before moving on in search of some other place for their winter or summer quarters. They lived, not in dark, deep grottoes, but in the shelter of cliffs and other natural shelters, where they could enjoy the daylight. Occasionally, they travelled to a specific place at the appropriate season, to take advantage of local resources. That is how the Magdalenians of the Eglises grotto, at Ussat, regularly returned upstream to the higher valleys of Ariège during the rutting-season of the ibex, when the salmon moved up to their spawning-ground or when the grouse came down from the higher slopes.

The rich legacy of artwork left by those men ranges from geometric carvings on assegais and animal figures carved in elaborate detail on propellers to pierced sticks in reindeer horn. The attention paid to such objects may have been due to the importance of their function: assegais

From the remotest to the most recent, the prehistoric peoples are richly represented in Midi-Pyrénées

An ibex pierced with lines, above two bisons, in the black room of the Niaux grotto in Ariege *(above).*

Black aurochs and mammoths, prehistoric animals painted in the Pech-Merle grotto in Lot *(opposite).*

Clay statue of bear, at Montespan *(right).*

A painted horse
and footprints
have been found
in the Niaux
grotto *(Ariège)*.

deteriorated rapidly; propellers increased the hunters' force and precision; pierced sticks were used to straighten out the assegais, lengthening their lives. These objects were thus vested with magical powers, hence the care taken in decorating them. Sandstone sculptures have also been discovered, as well as small engraved stone slabs: the latter have been found in more than twenty sites in Quercy and the Pyrenees (there were more than a thousand of them at Enlène). Unlike

Pierced sticks, propellers, assegais were vested with magical powers, hence the care taken in decorating them.

the cave paintings, such artwork was not intended to last indefinitely and was often destroyed or recycled after having been used.

Two of the main schools of cave painting are represented in Midi-Pyrénées. Quercy, Lot, Tarn and Tarn-et-Garonne offer some thirty decorated grottoes, the main ones being Cougnac and Pech-Merle. In the Pyrenees of Ariège and Haute-Garonne, there are seventeen decorated grottoes, which include Niaux, Trois-Frères, Tuc d'Audoubert, Portel, Montespan, Marsoulas. Gargas is situated in Hautes-Pyrénées, where

Pech-Merle (Lot) is unique for the wealth and diversity of the paintings on the grotto's walls. Shown here: red aurochs, which the hand of man has captured in flight and immortalised (left).

there are four others. The sites are often clustered together, as along the Volp, around Tarascon-sur-Ariège or at the junction of the Lot and Célé rivers.

The themes represented combine common features and local characteristics. Bisons are more frequent in the Pyrenees, aurochs and mammoths in Quercy. Engravings, paintings, line drawings in red or black abound everywhere. Some techniques are unique to Ariège. The same is true of the clay modellings found at Tuc d'Audoubert, Montespan, Labouiche and Bédeilhac. Engravings on clay ground are more common in the Pyrenees than anywhere else. Yet the stencilled patterns of bent thumbs found in Ariège (Trois-Frères), Hautes-Pyrénées (Gargas) and Lot (Pech-Merle) indicate that there were contacts between the various communities.

Archaeologists have identified a rite that recurs frequently. In a dozen of so decorated grottoes, bone splinters were stuck in cracks in the walls, for no apparent reason. The artists may have done this in the hope of getting in touch with the spirits on the other side of the cave walls. Beliefs of this kind would account for the fact that they pushed their way right into the deepest recesses, the darkest and furthest away from the cave entrances. They thought that those grottoes were home to spirits whom they believed controlled their world. By entering in the grottoes to paint on the walls and the ground, by carrying out rituals there, they hoped to act upon these forces and appease them. ■

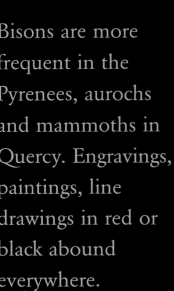

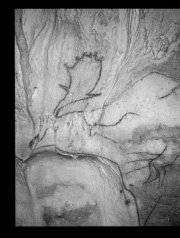

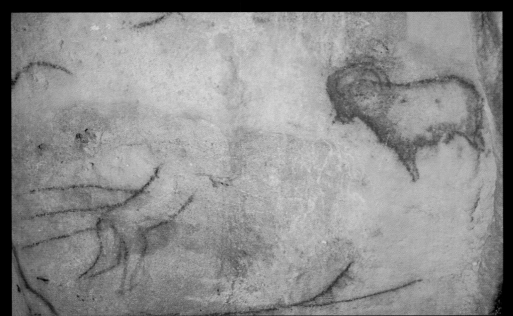

Bisons are more frequent in the Pyrenees, aurochs and mammoths in Quercy. Engravings, paintings, line drawings in red or black abound everywhere.

Reconstitution of a reindeer hunting scene during the Magdalenian era. This fresco by Gilles Toselo is exhibited at the Pyrenean park of prehistoric art at Tarascon-sur-Ariège *(left)*.

Another major site in Quercy: Cougnac grotto. A small figure pierced with lines faces a red ibex *(above)*. A second little man, with no head and pierced with arrows, stands below a red ibex, on a large megaloceros reindeer that curves round the cave wall *(opposite)*.

DOLMENS AND MENHIR STATUES

DATING FROM THE END OF THE PREHISTORIC ERA

Pottery found amidst human remains and objects of the Neolithic Age, in the grotto of Foissac, in Aveyron *(below)*.

Some 1500 or so dolmens have survived in Midi-Pyrénées. They are to be found mainly on the causses, the dry plateaux of Aveyron and Quercy, but also in the foothills of the Pyrenees, in Ariège. Most of these monuments now lie in ruins. They have given rise to picturesque legends, handed down by popular folklore, of huge stone tables: owing to erosion, all that survives in many places is the megalithic structure of barrows that were once entirely covered. These were communal graves, built above ground and designed to emphasize the bribe's or the clan's sense of community and territorial claims. Human remains have been found in these funerary chambers, besides decorative objects, flint weapons and potteries that date from the end of the Neolithic age (3500-3000 B.C.), the Copper Age (3000-2100 B.C.) and the beginning of the Bronze Age (2100-1700 B.C.). Current archaeological research has focused on uncovering and investigating more barrows in the region.

Menhirs are fewer. Their function is unclear. In the hills of Rouergue, the mountains of Lacaune and as far as l'Espinouse, more than a hundred carved standing-stones have been found, with patterns that give them an evident anthropomorphic appearance. Those in the distinct Rouergue style are among the earliest instances of monumental statuary in Europe and they are certainly the most richly documented ensemble of artwork from the earlier Bronze Age. Whether they were intended to represent tutelary divinities or dead clan-members who were worshiped as heroes, or whether they were symbols of a tribe's claims to a given territory, these standing-stones are an invaluable artistic heritage which raises problems of conservation. The finest are on show at the Fenailles museum at Rodez or at thematic sites at Brassac, Miolles and Murat-sur-Vèbre, in Tarn. Others have been left where they were found, after having been set upright again; unfortunately, they suffer from erosion and vandalism.

The recently restored dolmens of Pech at Saint-Antonin-Noble-Val, in Tarn-et-Garonne. The original monument, raised in the centre, is placed in a long barrow, with a second dolmen placed at the front *(above)*.

The La Peyre dolmen, at Vaour, in Tarn, in the course of being excavated. One can see the frontal stone of the barrow *(above right)*.

The Pierre Martine dolmen, at Livernon, in Lot. The covering slab-stone is 7 metres long and weighs several tons *(below right)*.

Menhir statues of Jasse du Terral, at Miolles *(Tarn)*. Left: statue of a male figure, with cross-belt, dagger, axe, bow and arrow. Right: statue of a female figure, one of the few to have a mouth, wearing a necklace with some pendant hanging between the breasts.

Legs are short, with feet hanging, which suggests that they are shown sitting. The man's legs are closed, the women's parted *(right)*.

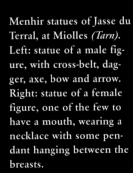

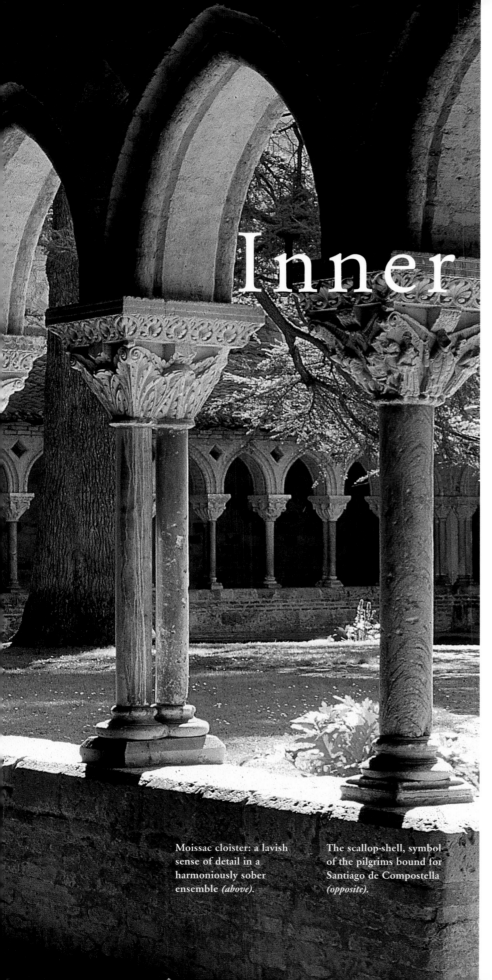

Denis Milhau
Art historian

Inner

light

NORMANDY, BOURGOGNE, AUVERGNE OR PROVENCE are all famed for their rich Romanesque heritage; yet, in order to steep oneself fully in that art and yield to its magic, Midi-Pyrénées is the region to visit. Far from being a merely administrative entity, it corresponds to geographical and historical realities, bringing together as it does the valleys from the south of the Massif Central and those of the northern slopes of the Pyrenees that converge on the Garonne river and open out towards the Atlantic and northwestern Spain. In its westward expansion, Christianisation swept across this region and pushed out as far as Spain's Cape Finisterre and Santiago de Compostela, which house the relics of Saint James, who carried the teaching of Christ to what at the time were the farthest shores of the western world.

Midi-Pyrénées has also preserved the memory of Charles the Bald's southern provinces of

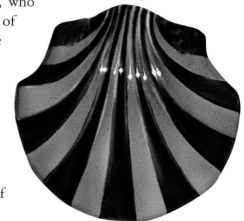

Moissac cloister: a lavish sense of detail in a harmoniously sober ensemble *(above)*.

The scallop-shell, symbol of the pilgrims bound for Santiago de Compostella *(opposite)*.

the Carolingian empire, where Christian civilization played out its confrontation with Islam. Moving up southwards along the Mediterranean and across the Iberian peninsula, Muslim invaders had tried to invade the southern provinces of the Christian world in a pincer movement.

The Romanesque art of Midi-Pyrénées was fashioned by the pilgrims' routes that took the faithful to Rome, Santiago de Compostela and other holy landmarks of medieval Christendom. It illustrates Christianity's growing confidence, as it won back territories lost to the Muslims, and the increasing stability of the populations that helped to shape the region.

Romanesque art creates a sense of wonder and testifies to the extraordinary impetus and talent which man put into shaping his environment. Romanesque art developed as feudal France underwent a wide-ranging reorganisation and benefited from a fresh impetus. Its beginnings coincided with the breakup of the Carolingian empire that resulted in the emergence of a feudal kingdom where absolute social and political supremacy was concentrated in the hands of Hugues Capet, while the Catholic Church reinforced its moral authority. Romanesque art developed in parallel to this evolution, which reached its climax under Philippe Auguste, who understood the importance of strengthening the unity and power of a kingdom that was woven together from feudal loyalties. That is why, besides being artistically uniquely creative, Romanesque art bears witness to the complex history of an emerging civilization which tells us as much about men as about beauty.

Romanesque art bears witness to the emergence of a civilization that tells us as much about men as about beauty.

St-John-of-Jerusalem's Church, known as Templar's Church, in the Aure valley *(above)*.

The square belltower of Axiat church, with openwork effect of a two-tiered arcature *(opposite)*.

Midi-Pyrénées was one of the main cradles of Romanesque art. The history of the 11th and 12th centuries, when the region's cultural identity was fashioned and its artistic and social life opened up to the outside world, is written in its stones. From the 19th century onwards, writers have marvelled at how, around the year 1000, a "cloak of churches" covered the Christian world, a cloak, it should be recalled, that was woven of fears and terror as well as of joy and uplifting emotions. The combined efforts of the three social orders, which consisted of those who prayed, those who fought and those who worked, resulted in that period being one of the most fruitful and decisive in the region's history. Romanesque churches, and churches with traces of Romanesque architecture, dot the countryside, from the uplands of Aubrac to the Central Pyrenees, from Quercy to the southern slopes of Cerdagne and southwestern valleys of Bigorre, mapping out a geogra-

Notre-Dame Cathedral, at Saint-Bertrand de Comminges. Its belltower, a 33-metre keep, is visible from miles around. In the foreground, St-Just-de-Valcabrère.

An uncluttered
sense of balance:
Romanesque art
in St-Sernin's
basilica, at
St-Lizier, in the
Louron valley
and in Sainte-Foy,
at Conques.

phy of rural communities and small towns as well as larger urban entities such as Toulouse and Cahors, whose networks of streets still bear the traces of this medieval expansion.

In Midi-Pyrénées as elsewhere, the Romanesque expansion took place in a feudal context. However rich they may seem, today's architectural remains are mere fragments of a building frenzy that took place in a context of demographic pressure and was encouraged by the expansion of techniques, knowledge and philosophical thought, in what Georges Duby has described as "the big takeoff".

Whether in remote rural entities ("vicus") or in the urban boroughs that emerged around parishes which later grew into city districts, human geography was fashioned by religious architecture. One reason was an upsurge of religious feeling; to erect a church was to build a home for God. It also had a community-building function, bringing together the three antagonistic yet complementary social orders of the medieval world in a common, idealistic project that transcended their human and political dimension.

A fresco of Mont Church, in the Aure valley *(opposite)*.

Sun and shade effects on the walls of the Cistercian abbey, at Escaladieu *(below)*.

Whether in remote rural entities or urban boroughs, human geography was fashioned by religious architecture.

The diversity of Romanesque art in Midi-Pyrénées is partly due to the rivalry and struggle for control of the dimes that marked relations between the feudal lords, the church hierarchy and the established monasteries of the region that variously depended on Cluny, Saint-Victor de Marseille, Citeaux and Clairvaux. It is also due to the fact that Midi-Pyrénées was a crossroads of pilgrims' ways and the stage both of attempts to push back the Muslim forces and exchanges between the main countries of Christian Europe. People moved around a lot at the time, for religious motives or to conquer new territories; in 1096 Pope Urban II called from Toulouse for a crusade to liberate Christianity's holy places: he was consecrating the Saint-Sernin basilica, a key religious landmark on the route to Compostela. The Counts of Toulouse, who had fiefdoms in Provence, took an active part in the crusades of the Eastern Mediterranean.

Detail from St-Sernin's basilica, Toulouse. Bas-relief in the ambulatory, showing Christ surrounded by symbols representing the Evangelists *(opposite)*.

The porch of Carennac Church. Above the door, an outstanding tympanum, dominated by Christ in Majesty *(opposite)*.

Stained-glass window of Sainte-Foy Abbey, at Conques, designed by Pierre Soulages, an artist from Aveyron *(below)*.

Christ in Majesty, a gold statue sparkling with precious gems *(above)*.

In addition to its outstanding Romanesque art and stained-glass windows, Sainte-Foy Abbey, at Conques, houses a brilliant collection of religious artwork featuring several items in gold plate. The most valuable item in the Treasury is a gold statue of Christ in Majesty, inlaid with gems. This fascinating statue and reliquary holds court over an exceptional collection (some forty items) of goldwork inlaid with jewels, tapestries and valuable textiles, which is the soul of the abbey: the building was erected as a shrine for these marvels of holy artwork. The Treasury is reached through the cloister and former refectory, and richly rounds off a visit round the buildings.

Pilgrimages, crusades, expansionist feudal policies, the anchoring of medieval life in its environment, all go a long way towards explaining the impressive energy and adaptability of the creative architectural and artistic forces of the time, in the stimulating context of the "big takeoff". The building was carried out by local populations of serfs tied to the area where they lived; the work, though, was overseen by a new class of men, architects or foremen, who, from one building-site to the next, from one region to the next, from west to east and back again, contributed to create that cloak of churches which favoured the emergence of another calling, sculpture, which moved from the rank of craft to that of an artform that is admired and venerated to this day.

The Romanesque art of Midi-Pyrénées is the receptive crucible of an art that was common to the whole of medieval, Christian Europe.

The feeling one has of a recognisable family of inter-related buildings and works of art is due to the fact that the Romanesque art of Midi-Pyrénées may be perceived as the receptive crucible of an art that was common to the whole of medieval, Christian Europe, while in return sharing its inventions and idiosyncrasies with other regions.

The domes of Cahors and Souillac cathedrals have common features with those of Périgord and Charentes. The invention of a lateral circulation for pilgrims along side-aisles or around the choir, as at Conques and Saint-Sernin, is the result of a history of exchanges with Auvergne and Bourgogne as well as with Saint-Martial's cathedral at Limoges and Saint-Martin's at Tours which, unfortunately, have not survived. The breadth and iconography of Moissac's cloister are an example of the development of cloistral art. The monumental, edifying entrances of Conques, Moissac, Carennac and Cahors emulated those of other churches in the region, which have since vanished, and inspired the artwork that progressively led to the early gothic royal gateways.

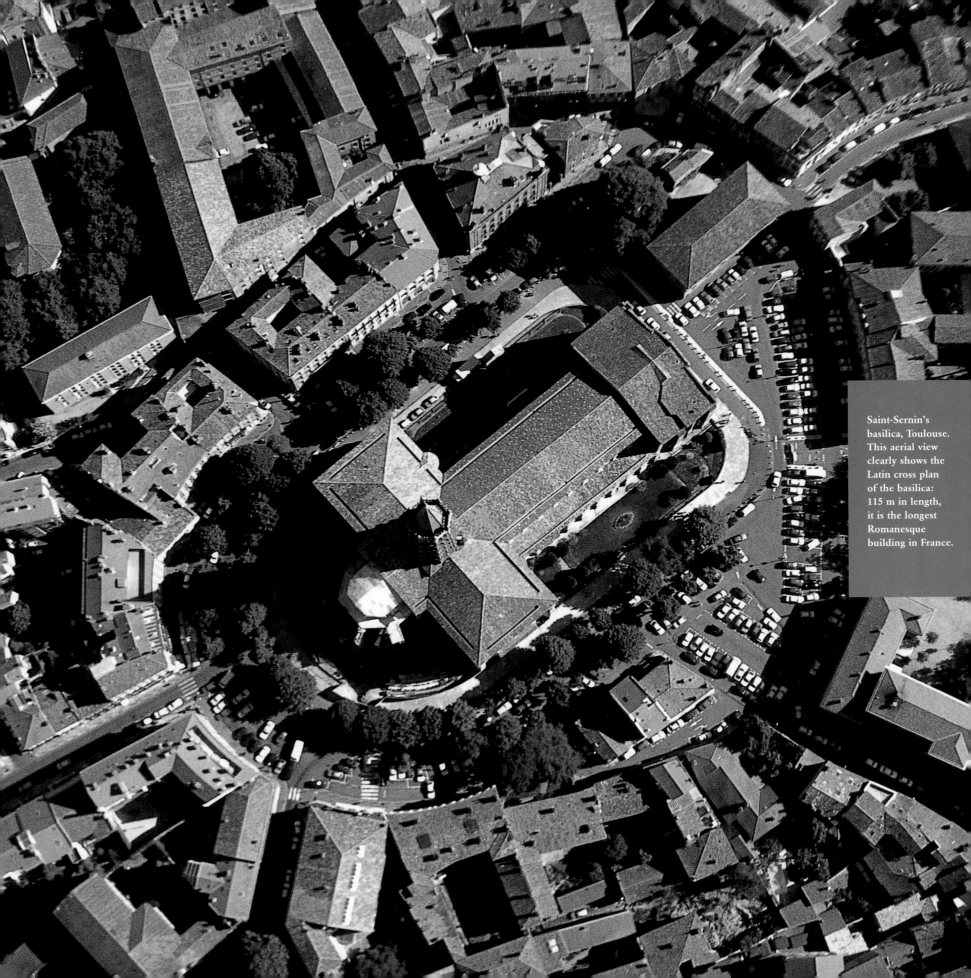

Saint-Sernin's basilica, Toulouse. This aerial view clearly shows the Latin cross plan of the basilica: 115 m in length, it is the longest Romanesque building in France.

The nave of Sainte-Foy de Conques. The white stonework is given a glow by the light that pours in through the admirably sober stained-glass windows.

Saint-Etienne's cathedral, Cahors. The keep-like bell-tower, with its cupolas, dominate the old city *(left)*.

The cupolas of Souillac's Sainte-Marie, capped with lanterns *(opposite)*.

Flaran Abbey. The chapter, with its clusters of fine columns *(below)*.

In the field of sculpture too, Romanesque art left an indelible mark. Midi-Pyrénées contributed to the emergence of carved figures. Moving away from an initially crude art-form that merely sought to illustrate religious texts, sculptors of Midi-Pyrénées gradually wrested out of their raw material human figures that celebrated their environ-ment and enacted heroic deeds in stories told in stone. In the remains of La Daurade cathedral, in Toulouse, as in the "Annunciation" carved on the entrances of Saint-Just de Valcabrère and Saint-Bertrand de Comminges, statuary that was hitherto a structuring, integral part of an architectural ensemble takes on a life of its own, providing early instances of an autonomous artwork that became fully independent during the Gothic period.

Romanesque art produced buildings that were human-sized havens of prayer and turned sculpture into an art-form whereby man felt authorised by Christ's incarnation to "be" and represent himself. So doing, Romanesque art emerged as an art of light, be it the inner light of thought and meditation that wells out of darkness, or the light of space, that structures matter, both the shelter-providing stonework and the transparency of stained-glass. Pierre Soulages's recent windows, at Conques, are a modern artist's tribute to the austere simplicity and spiritual atmosphere of Romanesque art, which spells out the simplest, deepest human aspirations and man's ability to set in stone his hope that the world he creates will reflect his human and humanist ideals. ■

Figurative statuary takes
on a life of its own,
heralding the Gothic period.

Gilles Bernard
Historian and geographer

A lesson in town-planning

THE FEAST OF LIGHTS, AT SAUVETERRE-DE-ROUERGUE: the central square is carpeted with twinkling candlelight; children are seated on the ground, fascinated by the thousands of flames that have transmuted the town centre into a milky way.

Pilgrims converge on the covered market of Beaumont-de-Lomagne for the foie gras season, to revere ducks and geese in this pillared hall of gastronomic worship.

Revel seen from the sky. The city is laid out in a hexagonal pattern, with the covered market-square in the centre, on which all the main streets converge.

L'Isle-sur-Tarn has a rich medieval heritage, with several timbered houses *(opposite)*.

On a sunny summer's day, a group of cyclists wend their way to l'Oustal de Valence, for an overnight stop, with a visit to Flaran in the evening, to explore the medieval *bastide*, or new town, across the river Baïse, built by Cistercian monks.

In the cool stillness of dawn, one can hear the clip-clop of horses down the streets of Cordes, the oldest of the Midi's bastides. Impossible to tell where the sound comes from, unless it be from some distant past…

Cordes, a bastide built for defensive purposes on the steep slopes of a hill in Tarn.

History seems to have stopped under the covered walks; the centuries mingle on the façades that line the squares. Somehow, the *bastides* defy time, as they hover on the elusive dividing-line between reality and dreamland. It is hard to imagine that they grew out of the struggle for power that was played out in this region, from the Mediterranean to the Atlantic.

When, at the beginning of the 13th century, the French, led by Simon de Montfort, reached Languedoc, they saw the rolling plains of the Garonne valley and hills of Gascony unfolding westwards. The Mediterranean *garrigues* abruptly ended at the level of what is today the Naurouze watershed, giving way to lush landscapes dotted with villages and farmsteads that seemed to beckon. Yet this paradise was, to the newcomers, a deceptive one, overrun by the heretical Cathar faith and ruled by noble families that had foresworn their oath of allegiance to the king. The local population had closed ranks behind the Count of Toulouse against the northerners, who did not even understand their language. How could one hope to restore the king's and Rome's authority without widespread destruction and massacres? Time was needed, a lot of time, and persuasive policies, that slowly took shape between 1220 and 1370 and can be summed up as follows: town-planning.

Under the leadership of Alphonse of Poitiers, Saint Louis' brother, and of successive royal seneschals, the French sought inspiration in policies that the Cistercians had experimented a century earlier.

From left to right:
The central square of Cologne, in Gers. The timberwork of the covered market rests on stone pillars.

Montesquiou, a bastide that opens onto the countryside of Gers.

History has stopped under the covered walks; the centuries mingle on the façades. Somehow, the *bastides* defy time.

Communities of monks had devoted their energies to laying the foundations of God's kingdom on earth, usually in remote areas, clearing away isolated valleys to build abbeys, with the buildings laid out in petals around a cloister. The cooperation between the monks and the king's representatives, begun during the crusade against the Albigeois, continued in Aquitaine, which was viewed as a land of spiritual reconquest.

The French chose to make the most of the weak chinks in the armour of Occitania: forests that had not yet been cleared and were hideouts for ruffians of all kinds, land seized from noble families that had been convicted of heresy. There was no question of conquering *sauvetés* (rural townships founded by monasteries) and *castelnaux*, fortified towns : the policy was to build towns alongside those that already existed and attract settlers to them. The purpose of these new towns, or

The covered walks of Mirepoix, Ariège, where it is so pleasant to linger.

Levis, a bastide erected on a hilltop overlooking the river Tarn.

The circular bastide of Fourcès, in Gers, with the most important flower-market in the South-West nestling in the centre *(opposite)*.

Grimacing faces sculpted on the timberwork of Mirepoix's covered walks *(below)*.

Sauveterre-de-Rouergue, a bastide in Aveyron *(below, right)*.

bastides, was to undermine the existing network of towns and villages, and encourage new loyalties, since the tithes and other taxes went directly into the coffers of the king of France, instead of into those of the local ruling families. Further to the west, the king of England followed the same policy, hence the network of *bastides* that also sprang up around Bordeaux and throughout Aquitaine.

The *bastides* of Occitania are quite different from the rural housing patterns of Provence. Settlements are much older, and larger, since they amount to medieval housing estates.

The sites chosen to build the towns resulted from chance rather than a deliberate, overall territorial plan. Their founders learnt to take advantage of every opportunity to create a *ville franche* (free town) or *vilie neuve* (new town), adapting the lay-out in each case, hence the fact that each of these townships is unique.

Differences are also due to topography and local building traditions, and the need, in some cases, to adapt existing habitations. Boundaries were dictated by rivers and forests; but there were common features. The town was usually built around a square, with streets branching off.

The population of the south-west was composed essentially of free men, who accepted to place themselves under the authority of a lord only insofar as he offered them protection and did not impose crushing taxes. Loyalties were ancient but fragile. What better protection could anyone hope for than the king's, since he had defeated the Count of Toulouse?

Each bastide is unique, owing to topography, local building traditions, and the need, in cases, to adapt existing habitations.

Like sirens beckoning from the hills on which they were built, the *bastides* lured peasants, tradesmen and shopkeepers into their embrace. Trumpet-bearing heralds were sent to neighbouring villages to announce the birth of a nearby *bastide*. Each family was offered a plot of land to build a house, a garden allotment and a field to grow cereals. Everyone

was considered equal: there were no serfs in the *bastides*. Every year, the heads of households elected consuls, who administered the community in accordance with the town's charter.

A certain number of privileges were listed in the charter, carefully meted out by the founders: too many privileges, and the *bastide* did not bring in enough income for its founders; too few, and people had little incentive to settle there. Another factor to be considered was the reac-

Lauzerte, also called the "Toledo of Quercy", is fashioned to fit the rock on which it is built *(opposite)*.

Autumn slips gently under the covered walks of Saint-Clar *(above)*.

tion of the local lords, who might be tempted either to offer their subjects incentives to try and prevent them from leaving, or to destroy the *bastide.*

In 150 years or so, the *bastides*, which were founded mostly in rich agricultural areas, had become market towns and overnight stops along roads and waterways, creating a network that enmeshed the former county of Toulouse. To the west, they interacted with the English townships on the royal chessboard of territorial ambitions that opposed the kings of France and England during the Hundred Years' War.

Some *bastides* – Villefranche-de-Rouergue, Mirande, Revel – proved to be instant and lasting successes. Others vanished without a trace. Most added to the landscapes a new generation of villages, alongside those that originated in the Roman era.

Detail of the beautifully-worked timberwork of a covered walk *(below).*

Down the centuries, the *bastides* forgot the circumstances in which they had seen the light and the word itself vanished, until the second half of the 19th century. This was the time of Walter Scott and Viollet-le-Duc: medieval keeps and cathedrals were a source of fascination; people imagined life in medieval castles, Esmeralda brought grace and youth to Notre-Dame-de-Paris. Everywhere, the Middle Ages had left enough traces to fuel the imagination, but it would be several decades more before historians realized that the *bastides* were still alive: the weekly market still took place on the central square, near old cereal scales, at a hub of straight streets pointing north, south, east and west.

At the end of the 20th and beginning of the 21th centuries, one no longer talks of towns, but of urban landscapes of roads and housing estates that to many are symptomatic of an impersonal, unnatural way of life, where everything goes too fast and has grown too big. As towns expand in uncontrolled fashion, people look back in nostalgia, hoping to find in the past answers to the despondency with which the future fills them. Heritage cannot, however, hold out promises for the future; all it offers is a mirage of ideals that occult present-day precariousness.

We seek refuge in old stones and traditions, hoping to escape the pollution of urbanisation in an untainted rurality where small was beautiful; the *bastides* seem to offer a perfect harmony, the combined charms of town and country. In fact, they should be remembered for their founders' boldness of vision and their first inhabitants' sense of solidarity. The *bastides* are much more than an architectural achievement; they are a testimonial of man's confidence in man. ■

The covered market-place of Grenade, with its magnificent timberwork. Markets, exchanges, gatherings of all kinds make of the market-place the throbbing heart of the town; the same is true of the covered walks of Mirepoix *(below)*.

Resistance down Sud

Claudine Pailhès
Archivist & palaeographer

CATHAR, ALBIGEOIS, PERFECT: those were the words used by the Roman Catholic church to describe the heretics of the Midi, who preferred to call themselves Good Christians. The Cathars were long perceived as heirs of Oriental Zoroastrianism and manicheism, but it is now acknowledged that their faith is a "radical version of the evangelist quest that marked the period", to quote the historian Anne Brenon.

A wave of spiritual aspiration swept through Christendom in the 10th and 11th centuries. People yearned for a faith that would bring them closer to God, truer to the ideals of the first Christians, who had preached poverty and non-violence; so doing, they rejected the Church as an institution, which they accused of having betrayed its mission, of being too rich, too close to those in power and too remote from the humble. Countless spiritual

Montségur Castle, a symbol of Cathar resistance, fell to the Royal and Catholic forces on March 2, 1244, after a harsh, yearlong siege *(above)*.

A miniature representing troubadours, who extolled a "courtly civilisation" based on mutual respect *(opposite)*.

In the 10th and 11th centuries, people yearned for a faith that would bring them closer to God and accused the Church of being too rich, too close to those in power and too remote from the humble.

Roquefixade Castle, which the Count of Toulouse and Foix regularly fought over, controlled a strategic position, between the County of Foix and Pays d'Olmes *(top).*

Preliminary sketch for *Les Hommes du Saint-Office,* by Jean-Paul Laurens, 1889. The all-powerful Inquisitor represents God's justice *(above).*

movements saw the day, many of them unstructured; some were absorbed into the Church, others were denounced as heretical. Among the latter were the Vaudois and those who became known as the Cathars.

What set the Cathars apart was their elaborate theory of dualism, which, even though it was anchored in the Gospels, was assimilated by Catholic theologians to the Manicheism of ancient Persia. The Cathars opposed the Kingdom of God to the world of Evil (mainly the world of the Catholic church, which hungered after power and riches), seeing in such contrasts the proof of the existence of two principles, Good, or the eternal God, and Evil, whence the material world and time originated. Souls were a part of the heavenly Being, some having "fallen" into the material world, where Evil trapped them in the human body. Once the body died, the soul passed into the body of another human being or, failing that, an animal, before being finally reunited in heaven with its spirit. At the end of time, all souls returned to God, while the material world became nothingness.

To become a Cathar, one had to be baptised; this ceremony, called *consolament*, consisted mainly in a laying-on of hands. The Cathars believed that a *consolament* received on one's deathbed meant that the soul would be reincarnated in the body of another human being who could hope to attain the status of Good Christian. Those who received it in their lifetime and became "Perfect" undertook to lead a life of prayers, fasting and sexual abstinence, to refrain from eating meat or killing any living being. Rank-and-file believers were expected to take part in the *melhorament* whenever "Perfect" were present, that is to say, to ask for a blessing and share holy bread. For the rest, they were expected to try and abide by the moral principles of the Cathar faith, one could not really consider them sinners, since they were victims of the Evil principle.

In the 11th century, the presence of Cathars was reported in several regions of the Christian world, in Greece, in the Balkans, in the Rhineland, in Italy, Flanders, Champagne, Aquitaine, at Orléans and Toulouse, where there were some as early as 1018. By the 12th century, the Cathar faith was very much present, and expanding rapidly. The faith proved to be especially popular in Languedoc. It was the dominant religion in Lauragais and very popular in Albigeois, the county of Foix, the Hers valley, in Razès, in the Corbières and Fenouillèdes. Gascony to the west, Narbonne to the east, marked the limits of the Cathar presence. To the north, Catharism was present in the Agen district and Quercy, while links between Foix and Catalonia took the heresy southwards, beyond the Pyrenees. As with any religion or set of mental patterns, a variety of factors explain the success of Catharism and how Languedoc provided a

In the 11th century, the "rock of Foix" was the residence of the counts of Foix, a powerful dynasty that was the heart and soul of the Languedoc resistance during the crusade against the Albigeois *(opposite)*.

favourable context where it could flourish. Social divisions were less marked in the Midi than in the north, ties between the ruling families, as well as between lords and their subjects, were less strictly hierarchical. Land and property were divided among the heirs: this gradually impoverished the nobility, and made the wealth of the Church all the more glaring, especially insofar as this wealth was achieved to a great extent at their expense, since their land was tithed. The ideals of a *courtly civilization* had encouraged the idea that true nobility was a matter of feelings rather than blood; troubadors were treated as equals, whatever their social background. The idea of an egalitarian religion was therefore extremely attractive. Moreover, the ability to live with "others", an easy sense of tolerance, were fostered by the presence of Jewish communities in several towns of the Midi, trading and cultural ties with Muslim Spain and exchanges with the harbours of the Mediterranean.

Hence the indulgence of the counts of Toulouse and Foix, the viscounts of Carcassonne and Béziers, who allowed the heresy to spread unchecked, whereas in the north of France, it was systematically resisted

The ability to live with "others" was fostered by the presence of Jewish communities, ties with Muslim Spain and exchanges with the harbours of the Mediterranean.

The battlements of Toulouse being raised by the city's inhabitants, who remained loyal to Count Raymond VI, by J.-P. Laurens *(above)*.

Saint-Félix-Lauragais, where the Cathars held their Council in 1167 *(opposite)*.

The number of Cathar converts was highest in the sprawling dioceses of Narbonne and Toulouse, in the Corbières, the Lauragais and the Ariège.

In 1215, the house of the Inquisition, place du Parlement, Toulouse, where the Dominican Friars judged heretics *(opposite)*.

by the secular authorities. The remoteness of the Roman Catholic Church's representatives also explained its success. The number of Cathar converts was highest in the sprawling dioceses of Toulouse, which reached as far as Razès, the Corbières and Fenouillèdes, and Narbonne, which extended to Lauragais, pays de l'Hers and Ariège. The bishops never visited such areas, where the Church was associated with illiterate priests and collectors of tithes.

The Cathar church of Languedoc was severely condemned by successive Councils, but it grew into a fully-fledged Church. In 1167, "Father" Nicetas came from Byzantium to preside over the "Council" of Saint-Félix-Lauragais, which institutionalised the Cathar communities and ordained the Cathar bishops of France (that is to say, northern France), Lombardy, the districts of Toulouse, Carcassonne, Agen and Albi. This event amply illustrates the spectacular expansion of the faith. In the early 12th century, the Cathar community was a visible part of society, with its hierarchy of Perfect, deacons and bishops, and communities of Perfect women. The faithful included several knights and lords of townships that provided sanctuaries for the *Bonshommes*, or Good Christians; there were Cathars among the most senior members of the Count of Foix's household; and the faith enjoyed the tolerant support of non-Cathar ruling families. To the Roman Catholic church, the situation was simply unacceptable. The breaking-point proved to be the murder of a papal legate by a squire of Raymond VI of Toulouse's retinue. Pope Innocent III promptly excommunicated the count and launched a crusade against the heretics as well as all those who protected them; he ordered that their land and belongings be confiscated and given to "good catholics". King Philippe Auguste refused to lead the crusade, but several barons from the north of France took part in it. In June 1209, the crusading army, which had followed the Rhone valley, seized the lands of Trencavel, viscount of Béziers and Carcassonne, and of Mirepoix. There followed twenty years of fighting, which was periodically interrupted by truces between, on the one hand, the crusaders led by Simon de Montfort then by his son Amaury and finally by the king of France himself, Louis VIII, and, on the other hand, the lords of Languedoc, who had closed ranks around the Count of Toulouse. Those twenty years were marked by the battle of Muret, where Peter II of Aragon, who had come to fight alongside the troops of Languedoc, was killed, by the 1218 uprising of Toulouse, which resulted in Montfort's death, by countless battles and sieges. The outcome was the treaty of Meaux-Paris, in 1229; northern Languedoc passed under the control of the royal crown, and the County of Toulouse suffered the same fate after Raymond VII's death. In 1242, lords who had had their lands confiscated rebelled and in 1243-1244, Montségur castle, the Cathars' last stronghold, was besieged and taken. Those were Languedoc's last attempts at resistance. What had started out as a religious issue had been exploited by the French crown and resulted in the military conquest and political annexation of Languedoc, at the expense of a local nobility that, by and large, was not Cathar.

In spite of the shelter and help provided by the local population, the Cathars were persecuted, arrested, burnt at the stake. In 1232, the Cathar hierarchy had proclaimed Montségur the "see and soul" of their Church, hence the symbolic significance and impact of the siege, the final defeat and ensuing pyre. In 1231, the Roman Catholic Church created a powerful and fearsome institution, the Inquisition, to eradicate the heretics. Even so, in the upper Ariège valley, Catharism made a comeback in the late 13th and early 14th centuries, which was finally stamped out by two inquisitors, Geoffrey d'Ablis and Jacques Fournier. The last trial took place in 1335. Catharism was dead.

Catharism was a religion, nothing more. It fell into oblivion before being rediscovered in the 19th and more especially the 20th centuries. The tragic facts of Cathar history were distorted for political, social and esoteric reasons, which included a support of Nazism. The mysteriousness of a distant, extinct religion and the dramatic fate of the Cathars' martyrs have contributed to fascinate a wide public that knows little about theology. The simple truth, though, is that the *bons hommes* were men of God. ■

Extract from the *Cathar Ritual* (13th c.), which is a translation of the New Testament into Occitan *(above)*.

Jean Négroni in the part of St Dominic, in Stellio Lorenzi's *Les Cathares* (1966).

A religious issue exploited by the French crown had resulted in the conquest and annexation of Languedoc, at the expense of a local nobility that, by and large, was not Cathar.

Sainte-Cécile of Albi: the cathedral was built in the aftermath of the crusade against the albigeois as a symbol of the Church's power.

OCCITANIA: *QU'ES AQUO?*
Occitania, what's that?

Jean-François Laffont
A scholar of occitan

> Enriched by its exchanges with the Arab-Andalousian civilization, the troubadour movement invented courtly love and extolled the nobility of the soul, known as *paratge*.

Occitania: the word is widely used, often wrongly, in commercial or touristic contexts which have little if anything to do with the civilization with which this relatively recent word is rightly associated. Barely a century ago, the word Occitania was coined by Antonin Perbosc to describe a region that includes Midi-Pyrénées. Should one infer from this that he also invented the Occitan language, literature and culture? Certainly not, even though there is no doubt that this founding act was followed by a renewed feeling of local identity and pride among the inhabitants of the Midi.

From an administrative point of view, Occitania straddles seven regions (among them Midi-Pyrénées), 32 "départements", 12 Italian Alpine valleys and the Spanish Val d'Aran, that is to say 190 000 km² and 13 million inhabitants... three million of whom daily speak Occitan. The language is in fact the main unifying factor. The Langue d'Oc appeared as early as the 10th century; directly derived from Latin, it rapidly became an important cultural factor of medieval Europe, since it gave birth to the philosophical and literary movement of the troubadours. That was the time when Occitanian civilization shone as a beacon in a divided, war-torn Europe, contributing in a major way to the history of humanity. It is currently a field of research and scholarship that is taught and studied in some hundred universities and about 20 countries. Enriched by its exchanges with the Arab-Andalus civilization, the troubadour movement invented courtly love and extolled the nobility of the soul, known as "paratge", as well as the ideals of tolerance and "convivencia". But those ideals, which marked a break with the overall social and religious context, also made for tensions: tolerance, and more especially religious tolerance, were deeply suspect in a period marked by successive crusades; it is worth remembering that, for thirty years, barons from the northern provinces overran Occitania in the name of King and Christ. The Cathars who lived in the region were branded "heretics" and exterminated, the lands of the Occitanian nobility confiscated and attached to the crown; the troubadours were no longer to be heard.

Even so, until the French revolution, Occitan remained the dominant language throughout the south of France, where very few people spoke French. The Revolution marked the official death of regional languages, French being used as a means of unifying a nation that was in need of soldiers and manpower. Occitan revived as a literary language thanks to the vibrant talent and personality of Frédéric Mistral, the author of "Mireille" and founder of the "Felibrige", or poetry jousts, who, in 1904, obtained the Nobel Prize for literature. A more recent wave of Occitanisme was ushered in after 1945, by people who had fought in the Resistance, with a whole new generation of writers whose works were read well beyond the boundaries of the region: Joan Bodon, Max Rouquette, Robert Lafont, Bernard Manciet, Félix Marcel Castan, Alem Surre-Garcia... Nowadays, when one talks of encouraging a Europe of regions, one finds in the Occitan revival a powerful stimulus and symbol for the other regions of southern Europe, that could encourage the emergence of a common outlook and cultural identity. Thus, while centralising, "northern" models are dreamt up in Paris and Brussels, a "Latin" Europe sharing a common culture seems to be taking shape, extending from Naples to Lisbon, and passing through Toulouse.

Occitania can thus be viewed as a prospect, an outlook, a set of values kept alive by a millennial language. Throughout Midi-Pyrénées and beyond, "calendretas" (kindergartens), primary and even secondary schools are springing up and attracting increasing numbers of eager pupils. Occitan drama is making a comeback, with companies and actors such as Carloti, Theatre de la Rampe, and Claude Arlang. Occitan music, too, is enjoying a revival, with groups and singers such as Fabulous Trobadors, Nadau, Massilia Sound System... Radio stations (Radio Occitania) and television channels (OC-TV, which is available on Internet on www.oc.net and via satellite) are making the language and culture part of our everyday life.

Félix Marcel Castan, whose vision of decentralisation goes well beyond the usual debates on the issue, sees the future along the following lines: "The survival of civilisation will come, not from national or regional entities, nor from regressive ethnical communities, but from a new way of life, a shared culture, consideration for one's environment, the coexistence of individual and collective aspirations. The future for Occitania lies in using its language and values to promote the future well-being of all mankind – an ambitious and fulfilling cause."

In Midi-Pyrénées, active community actions have developed in recent years. In 1998, a new movement was created, *Convergencia occitania*, which federates some 55 associations that work to promote Occitanian culture in Midi-Pyrénées and beyond. This has resulted in the emergence of many cultural programmes, on which there is a political consensus. In spite of their political differences, the city council of Toulouse, the General Council for the *département* of Haute-Garonne and the Regional Council of Midi-Pyrénées work jointly with *Convergencia occitania*: one project is to create an Occitanian cultural centre, or *Ostal d'Occitania* in Toulouse, that should give local culture a major impetus.

The blue gold of Lauragais

Florence Boudou
Journalist

Hôtel d'Assézat, Toulouse : a fine example of the extraordinary wealth of the city's pastel merchants *(above).*

Agranat: a blackish, granulated paste from which the dye is obtained *(opposite).*

IN THE 15TH CENTURY, THE COLOUR RED, hitherto associated with wealth and power, gave way to blue, matching a change in social conventions. The craze for this new colour metamorphosed Midi-Pyrénées into a near-legendary land of wealth and plenty, a land of "cocagne", to use the provençal name given to the balls of pastel leaves that provided the precious tincture. In a century, the pastel trade transformed this quietly rural region into an international trading-centre, opening up new trading routes, speeding up technical, architectural and social change. The "blue gold" that enriched a powerful minority of tradesmen was transmuted into the pink bricks of prestige: the town houses and country manors they built for themselves were proof of a new-found, albeit short-lived, prosperity.

Let's go back to the beginning and start with the plant itself, that yields its precious tincture only to those who know how to handle it. Pastel was already known in classical antiquity. In his Natural History, Pliny classified it as a variety of wild lettuce: "the fourth is used by wool dyers... It stops bleeding, cures gnawing, rotting or serpiginous ulcers... Drinking it is recommended for the spleen." The first to use pastel, originally known as woad (a Germanic word), were supposedly those whom the Romans called Barbarians. From Strabo, a Greek geographer, to Caesar, the cliché of the Barbarians daubed in blue was well worn. The Bretons, who did not know how to make cheese and ate their dead, were perceived as emblematic of the

> With its heavy, yellow soil and landscape of long, low hills, the area was a natural garden.

From left to right:
a field of pastel in bloom, in Lauragais. Vivid yellow competes with the gold of sunflowers, which are also grown extensively in the Midi.

The leaves, from which the dye is obtained, are picked at midsummer.

Barbarians. This is how Julius Caesar described them in the *War of the Gauls*: "It is customary for the Bretons to rub themselves with woad, which gives their bodies a dark-blue colour and makes them particularly terrifying in battle." To the Greeks and the Romans, blue was a colour to be avoided, since they tended to associate it with terror, hell and death. In painting, it was used to represent the sky and the mystery of infinity. The Latin word *caeruleus* was applied both to the dark-blue sea and the sky. This has been replaced in French and English by "bleu" and "blue" respectively, both derived from a Germanic word, and "azur(e)", from the Arabic. Until the 12th century, blue was despised as a "poor man's" colour. Then, in the 15th century, woad became pastel, a word used to describe first the colouring paste then the plant itself. Linné later redis-covered the Greek name, *Isatis tinctoria L.*, derived from the verb "to pol-ish", since the Greeks believed that the plant helped to smooth the skin.

Cleaned, crushed and drained, the leaves are pressed into balls called *cocagne*.

Crushed then mixed with stagnant water, or human urine, the *cocagnes* become *agranat*, the dyers' paste.

Hôtel Jean de Bernuy, one of the finest examples of the Toulouse Renaissance style, an eclectic mixture of Gothic, Italian Renaissance and the art of the Loire châteaux.

The vault of Albi's Sainte-Cécile cathedral, detail of a carved window at Hôtel de Boysson *(above)*, Toulouse, a window of Magrin château *(below)*, in Tarn, and the vivid blue of cloth dyed with pastel.

Pastel was cultivated in Midi-Pyrénées from the 13th century onwards. Under Philippe the Fair, dyers in the Midi tried to reduce exports/imports. As from the 14th century, the Albigeois and the Ariège valley became pastel-growing areas. The merchants of Toulouse did not control the production yet. Slowly, though, the status of the colour blue was starting to change. In the 12th century, it had crept subreptitiously into stained-glass windows and heraldry, and its economic value soared as it spread to clothing, where it gradually became the dominant colour.

Assézat, Bernuy... Monuments to the glory of their owners, these magnificent houses recall the paradise lost of the land of *cocagne*.

Statues of the Virgin Mary that had been clad in red and blue henceforth wore mainly blue, which also became the colour of kings and noblemen. Dyeing techniques improved.

The blue extracted from pastel hardly needed any fixing and did not fade in the sun, which accounts for its becoming a sought-after luxury item. Midi-Pyrénées specialised in the production of the plant, which required farming techniques more akin to gardening than to agriculture.

Pastel impoverishes the soil, which must then be left fallow for a year. The plant was grown in soil that was ploughed in depth several times before being smoothed over: clods were broken up with wooden mallets. Sowing took place from February to March, with the fight against weeds beginning almost immediately. The first lettuce-shaped clumps of leaves were picked around Midsummer's Night, in June. In the Midi, farmers could expect up to five crops, with regular controversies over the quality of the harvest. The leaves were cleaned and taken to the nearest mill to be crushed. Once all the juice had been drained away, the crushed pulp was rolled by hand into balls called "cocagnes" and left to dry, until quite hard. They were laid out to dry on wicker trays (only one is known to have survived; it is on view at the château de Magrin, in Tarn). The balls took a fortnight to dry.

Good-quality ones were heavy, dense and black on the outside; they were easy to store and transport, but had to be submitted to various chemical operations before being used for dyeing: *granar, banhar, virar,* grinding, soaking and stirring. The *cocagnes* were broken up and crushed; they were then mixed with stagnant water or human urine, the resulting mixture giving off a fulsome smell and toxic vapours. The whole process was carried out in the countryside. The end-result was

Before being left to dry, the pastel leaves are crushed by a huge millstone pulled by a beast of burden *(above)*. The only surviving example of a pastel dryer is to be found in Magrin château, in Tarn.

pastellum agranatum, used in the dyeing trade: it took about 400 balls of pastel to obtain 100 kg of powder, and a year elapsed between the harvest and the end-result, the actual pastel powder.

From 1500 to 1515, Lauragais was a major supplier of pastel. With its heavy, yellow soil and landscape of long, low hills, the area was a natural garden. "Of all the kingdom's regions, pastel grows best in Lauragais," wrote Olivier de Serres. Toulouse became the centre of the pastel trade. Testers experimented with dye samples. Official weighers weighed the plant. Dyers defined the strength of the pastel. All these different aspects of the trade took part in Toulouse. Sometimes, when the previous year's harvest had been good, the crops were sold *alarisc*, with no official auction. It was almost a game. As the pastel trade developed in Toulouse, trading routes developed towards Bordeaux, down the

From left to right:
Fashions come and go, elegance stays, and is timeless, like this bow-tie.

After a bucolic meal: a pastel tablecloth drying in the sun, against a background of green grass.

Garonne, since land transport was fifteen times more expensive. Exchange offices popped up all over Toulouse, since peasants only accepted cash payments. Money-changers paid out coins against bills of exchange issued in Lyons. Pierre d'Assézat traded everywhere: in London, Antwerp, Rouen, Bilbao, San Sebastian and Pamplona. A massive inflow of money financed the export trade and the inhabitants of the Pyrenees who had until then had the monopoly of the pastel trade were reduced to having to come and buy it in Toulouse. Palatial town houses were built, such as Assézat's or Jean de Bernuy's, for which 107,000 bricks were bought in two months: what remains of the building now houses Lycée Fermat.

Monuments to the glory of their owners, these magnificent houses bear witness to the paradise lost of the land of *cocagne*, which, however, did not last. A rainy spring in 1561 that brought on poor har-

At Lectoure, in Gers, in the home of a pastel-loving couple, as is evident from the hall furnishings.

Around Avignonet-Lauragais, where cereals grow just as lushly as pastel used to.

vests, the outbreak of the wars of religion in region and the competition of indigo, an exotic plant brought back by the Portuguese in the 16th century, all combined to bring this golden age to an end.

By the 19th century, there were only forty mills in Albigeois, out of the eight hundred there had been in the 18th century. The legendary plant of wealth and plenty enjoyed a brief revival during the continental blockade decreed by Napoleon against England, one of the main importers of indigo. In order to dye his soldiers' uniforms in blue, Napoleon encouraged the French to find other sources of dye. The prefect of Tarn, Pierre-Joseph Marie Baude, tried to revive the pastel trade

La Fleurée de Pastel, a boutique in the home of Pierre Delfau, Toulouse, that sells clothes and house linen.

around Albi and opened an experimental school in the city. Pastel was also grown in Aude. But the project needed time and Napoleon soon gave up.

The golden age of pastel left its mark on the region. To this day, it remains a source of local interest, as at Lectoure, in Gers, where a Belgian couple fascinated by pastel's deep blue has revived the culture of isatis, enabling it to make a comeback in sophisticated fashionwear: navy blue and black have become the hallmarks of elegance. Toulouse continues to oscillate between tradition and modernity: whereas a city like Rome was early on won round to blue, the colour pink continues to dominate the city architecture. The colour of the soil, it seems, is more highly-prized here than the colour and grace of cerulean blue. ■

Canal du Midi

A watershed of dreams

Pierre Le Coz
Writer

IMAGINE A WORLD WITH NO ROADS, a world in which men and goods travel along waterways – rivers, lakes, canals – a world where human activity is shaped by the direction in which water flows and dictated by topography.

Boatmen ruled over that world. In the south-west of France, midway between the Atlantic and the Mediterranean, each waterway had its flotilla of sailing barges and deal tubs, its community of bargemen, with their own laws and customs, its corporation of watermen. At school we learned that there were two kinds of rivers: those that were navigable and those that weren't. This would have made people smile at the time, since, once a river has tumbled down its mountain

Some hundred thousand trees have been planted along the canal. Most are plane-trees, but one also finds tulip trees from Virginia, cypresses and giant thuyas *(above)*.

In this 1818 sketch from the Navigation Archives, a boat equipped with a sounding-line measures the draught *(opposite)*.

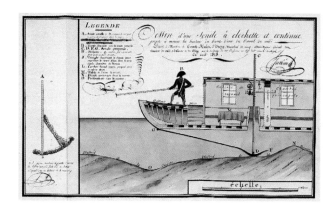

slopes and valleys, and reasonably slowed down, it becomes theoretically navigable. The only real obstacles are physical, such as when a rocky barrier or a riverless region comes between natural waterways.

The building of this new waterway magically tilted a whole land towards its western shore.

As Hegel put it, "Rivers bring people together, mountains separate them." And that, of course, is the case with the landlocked region that later became Midi-Pyrénées. Situated between the Atlantic and the Mediterranean, the region could, in theory, look both east and west – except that its network of rivers flows obstinately west, whether they originate in the Pyrenees or the Massif Central, bearing wealth and riches of all kinds to Bordeaux, Toulouse's hated and envied rival, situated at the end of the watery journey.

Bordeaux, though, faces the ocean, not the sea. It is built with its back to the sea, to that sea which lies to the south-east. In fact, the sea begins much nearer than one thinks, at the Naurouze gate, where the waters part company to flow east or west; it laps at the golden shores of ancient Septimania, which countless conquering armies criss-crossed.

In Midi-Pyrénées, the Mediterranean is both near and distant, a horizon which, to medieval and Renaissance man, shimmered with mirages of light, gold, blood and unknown sensual delights. For the Mediterranean opens onto another world, onto the wilderness of Africa, onto an imaginary East shaped by Biblical tales and the crusades. Hence the dream, a simple one, like all brilliant ideas, to create a route that would break the old curse once and for all, override geographical obstacles which oblige the region to look only west: the idea of a canal, a straight line that would link east and west, the Atlantic and the Mediterranean.

As one stands contemplating the green waters that flow down the narrow channel, it is hard to imagine the effort that went into making the dream come true. Pierre Paul de Riquet devoted his life and entire wealth to the project. He was not alone: countless labourers worked tirelessly on every inch of it, under the supervision of hosts of engineers who conceived and designed the complex system that, to this day, ensures that the canal never dries up. Others have described in lyrical terms this tremendous adventure, this project which to Riquet's contemporaries seemed on a par with the pharaohs' marvels. I shall not attempt to describe this all over again; instead, I should like to dwell on the canal's geographical and cultural impact, to suggest how the build-

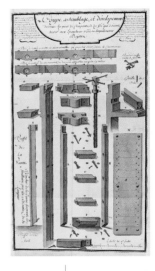

Drawing by Villacroze: wooden parts that go into the making of a regulation siphon *(above)*.

Pierre Paul de Riquet (bust by Griffoul-Dorval) devoted his life and entire fortune to making his canal come true *(above)*.

Where the canal begins: the Alzau offtake, where the Montagne channel begins. The river Alzau takes its source at Pas du Rieu, in the damp forests of the Montagne Noire *(below)*.

Over the years, several bridges have been renovated or rebuilt. The one a Donneville, between the Vic and Montgiscard locks, still has its original arch.

ing of this new waterway magically tilted a whole land towards its western shore and contributed to shape an identity that had until then remained little more than a vague dream: an identity that grew out of being at the crossways of sea and ocean. What happened therefore went well beyond the mere building of a canal: a whole new world opened up, a world that belonged to the realm of myth rather than reality was suddenly within reach.

In practice, this meant that, thanks to a tight network of countless waterways, the bargees of Lot and watermen of Tarn, Agout or Baïse, could henceforth travel to Sète or Narbonne – which, in fact, meant that they could travel even further, since one could then obtain a passage to Spain or Italy, North Africa or Greece, Egypt and the Holy Land…The

Life on the canal is regulated by those that travel along it and those who live on its banks, like this family of lock-keepers at Encassan.

gate between the Atlantic and the Mediterranean thus became a cultural gateway, a sharing of dreams between east and west. Surely, you will say, Pierre Paul de Riquet did not think of all that when he dreamt up his canal. Yet I am convinced that somehow, subconsciously, he was galvanised by the idea of making the region's aspirations less one-sided, of offering new

Myth-making and imagination are what drive men to attempt such feats.

horizons. Surely one does not devote one's lifetime and entire wealth to a project that has merely an economic dimension. Myth-making and imagination are what drive men to attempt such feats. Practical considerations come later, economic and geographical advantages are offered as alibis by their inventors so as not to be dismissed as madmen. A childhood dream is thus wrapped in an appropriate, sensible packaging that makes it acceptable to "rational" officialdom: after all, adults are merely children playing at being adults, aren't they?

The name and concept of a region called Midi-Pyrénées are sometimes contested. What signification do "Pyrénées" and the distant mountain range carry for an inhabitant of Lot or Aveyron? As for "Midi", doesn't it suggest the song of cicadas and a blue Mediterranean rather than the forests of Quercy or the austere Aubrac plateaux? Some people have suggested that our region should be renamed "Central Occitania", which is not much better, perhaps, except insofar as it does point to its centrality; but even that does not mean much. When one looks at a map, one is struck not so much by our central position as by our proximity to two opposed shores.

> What was lacking was a physical presence linking the waters of sea and ocean, two worlds, two aspirations.

The area covered by Midi-Pyrénées is a go-between, a topographical in-between-ness that, historically, granted its inhabitants a kind of geographical and spiritual precedence of the other peoples in the area (those of Aquitaine to the west, those of Languedoc and Provence to the east), until this precedence was torn to shreds by the tragically famous Albigensian crusade.

"Central Occitania" is central precisely because it is poised in space and time at a point whence other places, other moments in history, take on a profounder meaning. That must have been what the people of the Middle Ages obscurely understood here, which may have been why so many of them, perhaps, turned to the Cathar faith, in quest of some kind of secret predestination dictated by a holy sense of place. All that was irreversibly destroyed by Simon de Montfort and his army. Or was it? Possibly, the dream of a land anchored in the centre of the

The lock-keeper at Saint-Jacques bridge, at Moissac, on the canal that flows parallel to the Garonne, has seen countless barges go by. Others prefer fishing, a favourite activity with canal-lovers.

world lived on, deep underground, in the collective consciousness. It materialised in the shape of a canal which re-established the region at the hub. Poetically, spiritually, it had always been at the hub, despite the trials of history, but what was lacking was a visible sign, a physical presence linking the waters of sea and ocean, two worlds, two aspirations.

What I like is the idea of a destiny written in water, of an inevitable destiny borne first by the initial mountain spring then, down-

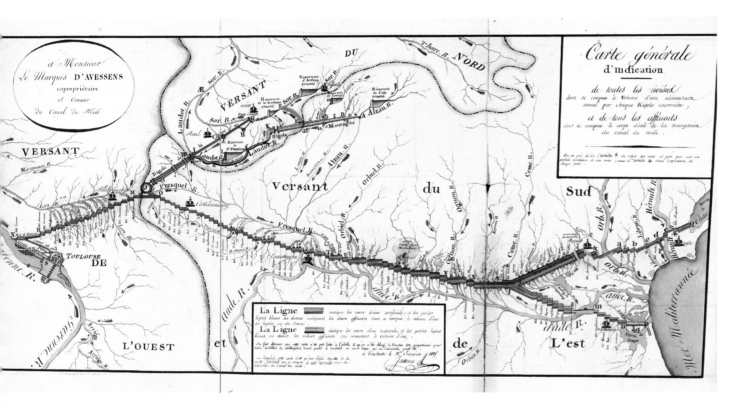

Map of the canal du Midi by Jasserieu, 1825: one can see the locks, the contours, and the rivers and tributaries that supply water for the canal *(above)*.

Ringed with pine-woods, Saint-Ferréol lake looks as if it had been designed mainly for bathing and sailing. Its dark surface is dotted with white sails in the summer, giving it the appearance of a tourist centre. Yet it was originally built for technical purposes, to provide water for the summit level of the Canal du Midi and avoid too great a difference between the highest and lowest water steps. The 67-hectare reservoir is enclosed by a massive dam that, to the west, closes the Laudot valley. A channel continues beyond the dam, below which an artificial waterfall sends rainbow sprays of water. Art and technique come together here as they do all along the canal, which has been designated world heritage by UNESCO.

valley by the flowing current, a destiny that the rivers simultaneously ignore and challenge, rebelling against the regions and men who attempt to tame them and to channel their shifting moods and currents. Caught in that constant struggle, man learns to shape a world "poised in time and space", as mentioned earlier. Yet, through something as simple as the building of a canal, that inevitable destiny suddenly seems suspended, magically circumvented. Which is why my intuition is that Riquet did not only make an old dream come true, he somehow tuned in to the spirit of our rivers, by offering them the possibility of wending their course south-eastwards and no longer merely westwards. ■

The channel of
La Plaine, which
brings water to the
Naurouze gate.

The barges
docked at
Toulouse's Pont
des Demoiselles
illustrate an
idiosyncratic
art de vivre.

Paths of

nature

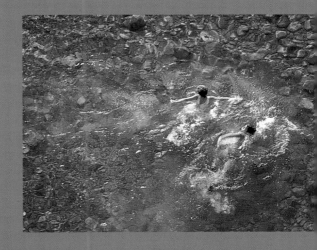

Yves Rouquette
Writer

The island on the roof of the world

DESPITE ITS HUNDRED AND ONE DIFFERENT TITLES the *causse* is one entity, and one to which I shall be a stranger till my dying day. It would take more than a few pages to give you some idea of this huge, landlocked continent, as multi-faceted as it is united, as exposed as it is secret. And this despite the fact that I have so often dreamt of it and travelled through it, and that some of my dear ones have ended their days there.

It is inhuman in its dimensions. It extends over the immense depression in the centre of the Massif Central which was occupied by the sea in the secondary era. As Patrick Bard[1] says, for millions of years, and through a depth of hundreds of metres, millions of tonnes of shells and shellfish, corals and submerged continents of mud and mother-of-pearl were deposited here.

From the Cévennes to Rouergue, from Margeride and Aubrac to Bas Quercy and Lomagne, the *causse* is as

On the blustery Sauveterre plateau, squat little houses merge into the mineral landscape *(above)*.

This golden thistle acts as a barometer. Its bracts unfurl when it is dry and close up again in wet weather *(opposite)*.

vast as the sea itself, and, bristling with reefs, can be calm or driven by the wind into long undulations. As over the sea, the wind rages unhindered, even by rocks; with the help of the frost and the rain, it gnaws and sculpts the limestone, forming camels and sphinxes, dogs or triumphal arches, dragons and knights, fairies or witches, even, in places, ghost-like towns: Montpellier-le-Vieux, Roquesaltes, Mourèze or Nimes-le-Vieux.

The heart of the *causse* is in the regions of Midi-Pyrénées, Aveyron and Tarn, but it extends as far as Lozère, Lot-et-Garonne, Hérault and Gard. Vultures circle the gorges of the Jonte and the eagles of Bonelli make their nuptial flights above the cirque de Mourèze. The dolmens of Saint-Affricain in the Sauveterre and Méjean *causses* are paralleled by the cromlech of the *causse* of Blandas, restored with magnificent impudence by Adrienne Durand-Tullou, the most rationalistic of witches. As ethnologist, botanist, archaeologist and speleologist, she was to her territory of Rogues and Campestre what the novelist Paul Gayraud[2] was to the *causse* of Séverac with his astonishing explorations of the depths of the human soul, written in the *langue d'oc*.

It has always given me immense pleasure to read their work and equal pleasure to count them among my close friends. I owe to them – even more than to Auguste Guiraud and Guy Tarlier[3], who struggled to preserve Larzac for the sheep – my passionate love of the plateaux and my affection for those who live there.

Earlier I used the adjective "multi-faceted", a term which so accurately describes this piece of our planet, unchanging but never the same, scored and cleaved by rivers to the point of being an archipelago.

The space between the islands is so narrow that Gargantua and Grangousier could shake hands across the abysses that separate the *avant-causses* from Larzac, the *causse rouge* from the *causse noir*, Auveterre from Méjean and the *causse* of Séverac. As one approaches Comtal and the *causses* of Villefranche, Villeneuve, Saint-Antonin and Gramat, the relief becomes gentler and life easier.

In the *Grands Causses*, which are forever obliged to turn their back on each other, water has decided everything, from life-style to territory. After sleeping and prowling beneath the carapace of limestone, and cutting its teeth in the bowels of the earth, it emerged into the open air via a passage which has enlarged steadily throughout the millennia.

A passage initially narrow, with gorges and ramifications, across which, as between Gibraltar and Morocco, the authorities have renounced erecting a bridge. (So much so that the language of *Occitan*

The space between the islands is so narrow that Gargantua and Grangousier could shake hands across the abysses.

A picturesque site in Cantobre, situated on a dolomitic bastion overlooking the gorges of the Dourbie *(opposite)*.

A landscape characteristic of the Gramat causse in Lot, one of the *Grands Causses'* many cousins *(below)*.

refers to the gorges of the Tarn as the "Tarn columns", rather as one talks of the columns of Hercules.) Then the gorges broaden, the gullies become coombs and the coombs become plains. Limited plains, still bounded by cliffs, but containing gardens, pasture land, orchards, villages and towns. Small towns. For on the heights there are no cities. Very occasionally, along the ancient roads, market towns. Otherwise hamlets and imposing, isolated farms which seem to ignore each other, although this is an illusion. The towns are in the valleys and those who live on the

The farm of Roques Altes in the *Causse Noir*. The earth owes its reddish colour to limestone decomposition *(above)*.

plateaux have always had to reach them by steep, tortuous slopes whenever they wished to do business or (before the advent of the press, radio or television) learn about what was going on in the world, make a match or leave the area. These towns are justifiably proud of their prosperous past, and are preparing for the future. Millau, capital of the *Grands Causses* and famed for its glove-making, vaunts the pharonic viaduct it is erecting; Villefranche de Rouergue, a striking walled town with a fine rural market, has in its collegial church the finest misericords of the great sculptor, André Sulpice; Cahors is famed for its wines, its attractive

A *gariote*, also known as a *cazelle*, in the Comtal causse. It was used as a shelter by shepherds or to keep hens, sheep or pigs *(above right)*.

81

The village of Pagnac, in the gorges of the Tarn. The smoke rising from the chimneys conjures up the blazing hearths of these thatched cottages.

A pair of wild vultures.
Like most birds of prey,
they had disappeared
from the *causses*.
They have now been
reintroduced into the
gorges of the Jonte in
Aveyron, and move
around following the
charnels placed for them
(below).

bridge and its domed cathedral; Souillac possesses a museum of automata which is almost as fascinating as the dancing Isaiah on the tympanum of its church…

To forget the charm of these towns, and of others lying below the plateaux, to concentrate on the high "deserts" and the tragic, silent nature of the great solitudes, is to reduce enjoyment of the *causse* to a consumer asceticism which the *Caussenards* themselves have never felt happy with.

A city like Millau, for example, has only been the starting point for excursions to the gorges of the Tarn, the Jonte and the Dourbie, the amazing pothole at Armand, or the caves at Dargilan since the coming of tourism. Before that who bothered about ascending these wild, increasingly inhuman defiles, so impressive in summer, so sinister in wintry weather? Who took pleasure from the desert? As holidays come to an end, people only carry on living there because they have to, as in any place where camp sites, hotels and nautical centres have closed, leaving only pasture land, a school, sometimes a grocery, butchers, bakers, passing postmen…

Millau, on the other hand, is a place to which people have always gravitated from all parts of the five great *causses* to find work. Formerly this involved producing tiles or *Graufesenque* pottery, examples of which flooded the Roman Empire before the industry was shifted (an early example of this policy!) to Arvernes at Lézoux where labour was cheaper. Then came the wool- and leather-craft industries, which are now in a par-

Harvest festival at
La Capelle in the
Sauveterre *causse (top)*.

The Tiergues dolmen.
One of the most
impressive megalithic
monuments of Rouergue
(above).

lous state. The same towns that attract natural resources, labour, intelligence and enterprise in prosperous times become points of departure in times of crisis. Formerly this was by train; now the motorway means that Millau is one hour from Montpellier and two hours from Toulouse…

Ah the roads! Almost as surely as the valleys before them, the great roads of the *causses* have criss-crossed the area, drained off men and led to the creation of the few small towns set up on the plateaux. Along their length, especially along the road which goes from the Domitian way at Rodez and beyond towards Arvernes, Gabales and Cadurques, all facilities for eating, drinking, sleeping and conducting business have been installed for the convenience of hauliers and travellers. For centuries upon centuries salt, wine and oil have been transported along this

The great roads of the *causses* have criss-crossed the area, drawn off men and led to the creation of the few small towns that exist on the plateaux.

Left to right:
This stoned pond, or *lavogne,* conserves that most precious commodity, water, and serves as a watering hole for sheep.

Roquefort cheese is refined according to an age-old tradition.

A field of blossoming narcissi sets the *causse* ablaze.

route in one direction; in the other direction went metals, resin, wool and the slaves needed first by Greece, then by Rome.

The towns that exist in the *causse* are also sited along this road: Caylar, La Cavalerie, Séverac. The monks of Marseille built their abbeys and priories – Benedictine, Grandmontine, Cistercian, Augustinian or Templar – along this axis. We must also not forget the sacred places of the Order of the Temple and the Hospitallers at La Couvertoirade, Sainte-Eulalie-de-Cernon, La Cavalerie and Saint Jean d'Alcas and the Viala of Pas-de-Jaux. What an immense power of attraction. But for real delight, one can go from surprise to surprise in the valley of the Dourbie, for example from Saint-Véran to Saint-Martin-du-Vican, passing through Cantobre, les Cuns, Nant and Saint-Jean-de-Bruel. There you will find Roman art in all its perfect humanity. And if you want to see Christ at his most loving you will find him in another *causse,*

Comtal, not far from Rodez. He hovers between four stars in the circular canopy over the well at Caysac, so beautiful, so peaceful and so tender that you would almost like to have been baptised there... It was inevitable that the A75 motorway would empty the main road through the *causse*, but it is sad even so. Now there are only long, straight lines, sleeping villages and impressive buildings left to bear witness to the intensity of the traffic which took this route through the *causse* for thousands of years, north to south and south to north, mingling lines of mules, herds being taken for summering or to the abattoir, men on foot or on horseback, in carts, in carriages or by car, going from feeding place to feeding place, from inns with huge stables to coaching houses.

I do not belong, either by birth or by family, to this *causse* of the past and of today, and, although I have explored it widely, I have never

Left to right:
A disc-shaped stele in the Templar cemetery at La Couvertoirade.

Remains of a troglodyte castle at les Baumes in Larzac.

A shepherd's shoulder bag in the making. Leatherwork is just one of the crafts practised in the *causses*.

lived there. When I was six years old (I'm now sixty five) the only thing I knew about it was its name, *causse*, which referred to the grey iron barrier bounding the red and green hills of Camarès to the north and east, this Camarès from where I am now writing, as the February snow whirls before my window. I was with my grandfather, watching over our twelve sheep and two goats in the neighbour's field. This huge wall intrigued me: "Grandad, what's that blue thing behind Gissac, behind Montaigut?"

"It's the *causse*, and Larzac behind."

I would have liked to know what was behind that again.

I imagined an enclosed orchard like that of our neighbours in Cayla, but huge, similar to the one with the four rivers alongside in which my Sacred History showed Adam and Eve lying in the grass between lions and does.

"Have you been there? What's it like?"

He had never been anywhere, not even to the army. Only to a few farms to look after the sheep for the year; to fetes in the village where, before being barred by the constabulary, he and his five brothers had spread panic with knife and stick; and to Lourdes with his wife – I have the photo.

As for Larzac, he knew that corn was grown in never-ending fields and that the sheep were "always white, because the earth there is colourless". He pointed at Loubière, beyond Gissac:

"It must be a bit like that, only bigger. A high plain with stones

In the Méjean causse rocky debris is scattered over the bushy *lande*. The wind reigns over these barren spaces *(opposite)*.

and grass growing through, big beautiful fields, and no springs; each house with its own water tank. That's what people say who've been to the manoeuvres at La Cavalerie."

"To be cavalry soldiers?"

"At one time, I suppose. La Cavalerie is the name of a village now."

"A village of horsemen?"

"Perhaps." He supposed so. He didn't really know.

Forty years later, at the Montaigut castle, just ahead of the *causse* I used to ride through on a moped with the Burési brothers from the cirque de Navacelles, or from Malène where my pal Albouy went to school and passed the time as best he could by reading, playing *belote* in the cafés and engaging in long drinking sessions, and again with the peasants and *maos* in the seventies, I met Pierre Gabane. He is a primary school teacher of encyclopaedic knowledge, collector of lightning

The Massif Central, a geological fragment of the old Hercynian chain of mountains, is the largest massif in France, extending over an area of 85,000 square kilometres. Its peaks are modest and the dominant impression is one of a plateau scored by countless streams – including the Dordogne and the Lot to the west – sometimes forming deep ravines, such as the Jonte and the Tarn gorges in the *Grands Causses*. The name Massif Central is of relatively recent, scientific origin; it was coined by two naturalists, Dufrény and Élie de Beaumont, who identified a geological unity in a great number of regions including the northern parts of Midi-Pyrénées. Aveyron, in particular Ségala, Lévézou and Larzac, and Tarn, with the Lacaune hills and the incredible bestiary of granite boulders at Sidobre, are both within the perimeter of this massif. Further south, the Montagne noire backs onto the powerful range which also brushes up against Lot's eastern flank.

Laguiole is as reputed for its knife as for its cheese, a *tomme* made from cow's milk. It is at La Couvertoirade that *perail*, a full flavoured sheep's cheese, is produced.

In the time of the Crusades, the Templars bred fighting horses at Larzac. Hence the name of La Cavalerie given to their vice-commander's residence.

stones, discoverer of collapsed dolmens, Neolithic villages and Visigothic necropolises:

"On the *causses*, where now the desert touches the sky, there used to be pine forests. For a long time people got wood, resin and pitch from them. Where sheep now graze and corn grows, herds of horses would run wild. This was before History as we know it, which is nothing. Men hunted them to eat them, not yet thinking of mounting them or harnessing them to a plough or cart. In the time of the Crusades, the Templars bred fighting horses at Larzac which would be taken as far as Palestine…Hence the name of *La Cavalerie* given to their vice-commander's residence."

He put his hand on my arm:

"Those wild horses, the warhorses, sometimes I see them at night in my dreams."

So do I. Sleeping or waking I have from time to time dreamt of the *causse* completely covered in pine forests and wide clear areas in which I see mustangs galloping between the juniper trees. My wild west, if you like.

But if I love it so ardently, it is because I picture the men and women who made it and who continue to forge its character, even as far as its harshest solitudes. The relative solitude of Comtal, full of country houses and farms built like forts surrounded by ploughed fields. But equally the deep solitude of Méjean, so mineral from one end to the other that the houses are built without frames or planks; here, more than anywhere else, the innermost depths of the soul are explored. In Méjean, abandoned corn mills stand like lighthouses, cowsheds look like cathedrals, houses are enormous scaly animals showing only their eyes and

A landscape typical of Larzac: high limestone plateaux and peaked cliffs award the traveller with a sensation of open spaces *(above).*

teeth to squalls and scorching heat, and millions of tiny flowers grow humbly, scarcely scented and yet endowed with a fairy-like beauty: dwarf irises, *parnassies* of the Great North, cardoons and the fascinating witch's, virgin's or angel's hair…

Over thousands of square kilometres, the sky, the earth, the elm trees killed by an epidemic, the wheat fields which we mowed in 1974 for the Third World as far as the Rajal del Gorps, the cemetery and the church of Saint Martin du Larzac, the wild fowl, the herds of cattle, the frescos of Villeneuve or Bozouls, the smoke from the squat chimneys, the sound of chain saws in the *causse noir*, everything in the *causse*, even man, speaks the language of the finite and the infinite, particularly at dawn and at dusk: that God is the world and yet he is not in it, as my brother Jean, who took on the name of Larzac well before the struggle

of the pacifists, stated in a magnificent poem. And so I am not surprised that after such a history of eccentric followers of God, it should have been on the *causse* that the Buddhists decided to establish their lamasery and receive the Dalai Lama and that Lanza del Vasto set up his Arc of joyful non-violence, that the orthodox should live there as cheesemaker-orants or that the Baillons should display the mysteries of glass, wool and leather at Brouzes, or even that, in Costes-Gozon, Débru should produce amazing, kindly monsters from metal.

One is on the roof of the world here, almost totally alone and exposed to all currents of thought, to the fullness of space and the secrets of the heart. One catches oneself hoping that the sky is not emptier than what appears to us on earth a desert. Experiencing eternity from here below, one almost begins to believe in it up there. ■

1. Patrick Bard: photographer and writer, author of *Causses*, éditions Freeway.

2. Paul Gayraud: Occitanian writer living at Séverac-le-Château, author, notably, of *Lo Libro del causse.*

3. Auguste Guiraud and Guy Tarlier: peasants of Larzac now deceased, who participated in all the battles against the extension of the military camp.

On the feast of Saint Urbain (25th May) the herds leave the plains of Languedoc to "climb up to Larzac". They come down again for the feast of Saint Géraud (13th October).

Claude Rivals & Pierre Espenon
Ethnologist and geographer

Gone with the wind

"THE ALL BLACKS CAME AS FAVOURITES. But there was one thing the New Zealanders had not counted on: the wind. A terrible, awesome, fantastic east wind, the *autan*, making the mid-November day seem like spring, with a high temperature and superb sunshine. The wind was enough to blow the horns off all the chamois in Ariège and the roe deer

Firmly attached to the line, the washing, buffeted by the wind, is dry in a flash *(above)*.

Either you love or hate the *autan*, said to drive women, men and beasts mad *(opposite)*.

A cornfield near Castelnaudary under the watchful eye of a scarecrow. This is where the *autan* of Haute-Garonne stops and the *marin* of Aude begins.

in the forest of Bouconne." Were these the wild dreamings of a febrile imagination, or the pertinent observations of a conscientious observer? However it may be, this is how the *Dépêche du Midi* reported the victory of the French team in the Toulouse stadium, on November 11th 1995. The east wind, called *altanus* ("of the high sea") by the poet Ausone,

The east wind, called altanus ("of the high sea") by the poet Ausone, because it originates in the Mediterranean, plays to a home crowd over a good half of the Midi-Pyrénées region.

because it originates in the Mediterranean, plays to a home crowd over a good half of the Midi-Pyrénées, its chosen region. Its domain extends precisely from Castelnaudary, where it arrives full of spirit, to Toulouse, then Valence-d'Agen, where it finally breathes its last breath. Nearer to the Mediterranean, it changes its name and its face: for natives of Aude it is the *marin*, which Ambroise Paré used to say gave the Narbonnese "their coarse, bleary appearance".

People around Toulouse never tire of discussing the east wind, to which they attribute in turn good or bad intentions, humour, malice, anger... Popular conceptions are all the more current because, despite numerous scientific investigations, the east wind resists all simplifying analyses. It is violent, excessive, incomprehensible; a real headache for meteorologists and an embarrassing guest for the inhabitants of Midi-Pyrénées. For whilst it can overturn the outcome of a rugby match in favour of the Red and Blacks, it has also overturned a train full of passengers, causing one death and eighteen wounded. This was in 1916, as the train was coming out of Revel station.

To live in Midi-Pyrénées (or especially in the Lauragais plains where the effects are tenfold) is to live with the excesses of Aeolus: twisted trees, roofs blasted with heavy stones, facades windowless on the eastern side all bear witness to the effects of the east wind, the *autan*. René Soula, who writes in Occitan, tells the story of Batiston, who was gassed in 1914 and who cursed the *autan* because it irritated his throat. "*Puta d'auta, puta de guerre*" was his favourite oath. In order to ward off this scourge which frightens the animals, affects the harvest and spoils the pig-slaughtering celebrations, the peasants of Terrefort brandish adages like screens. Words which try to forecast, speak of harvests, of cattle and of people's moods: "North wind corn, east wind wine"; "East wind today, rain tomorrow"; "When the east wind blows, don't take the

Animals start to become nervous even before the wind starts blowing *(left).*

Roofs are weighed down with stones to prevent tiles being snatched away by gusts of wind *(above).*

cows to the fields", or again "When the east wind blows, the madmen of Albi dance". The *autan* is also blamed for certain health troubles: rheumatism, headaches, and cardiac trouble – the effects of atmospheric pressure, degrees of humidity, ionisation of the air? The Toulouse psychiatrist Michel Escande offers another theory: "General belief in the harmful effects of the east wind on the nervous and mental functions of people is a factor in the causation of psychosomatic troubles." In other words, it's all in your head! Not so simple…

In this rush to vilify the east wind a not insignificant detail is ignored: it only blows 90 days per year, i.e. only a quarter of the year! This statistic which was established for the first time in the fifties by daily readings in the meteorological office of the estate of Roquefoulet at Montgeard was greeted with incredulity at the time. But in face of the strength of the established data, people had to concede.

The dominant wind is not what once it was thought to be and it does not explain the system of winds. Experience has shown that it is the west wind which has the lion's share of activity, with 240 active days per year. Even so they forget its name – the *cers* – and refer to "*lé véat*", the wind. The Toulouse and Lauragais regions are particularly subject to alternating winds: in Occitan one talks of the weather changing to the *autan* or to the *cers*, and a local place name one encounters frequently is "*Virevent*" (changing wind). So one can understand why shutters bang one way and then another when the wind is changing. Another belief that has been undermined is that the east wind brings rain; this is only true roughly one in ten times. By playing with words people can argue that it does in that it precedes the west wind which bears the rain from the Atlantic. The demise of the *autan* is concomitant with the arrival of the *cers* which, after the ballet of the shutters mentioned above, sheds its charge of water.

In our medium latitudes where the dominant winds are those which come from the west, and so from the Atlantic, the *autan* is contradictory, since it blows from the east and its immediate origin is the Mediterranean. Because of this it bears a certain charge of warmth and humidity, which varies according to the area and the type of *autan* it is. Its average speed is between 30 and 37 km/h, in other words about 20 km/h less than that of the *mistral*, which Meridionals are inclined to use as a reference. But the people of Midi-Pyrénées can point to the remarkably gusty nature of the *autan*. Its territory includes a sector to the east of Toulouse – that of the *autan violent*, the speed of which often exceeds 58 km/h. Within this sector it is in the zone bordering the north face of the Montagne Noire, in the plain between Revel and Labruguière, that the most devastating squalls regularly occur.

Another striking aspect of the east wind is the way it affects temperature. Globally, it causes a rise in temperature that contributes to the perception of the Toulouse climate as temperate. And yet there is a type of *autan*, called the Siberian *autan* (or *auta fret* in Occitan), which causes

The average speed of the *autan* wind is about 20 km/h slower than that of the mistral, but it whips its way through the Haute-Garonne corridor (*left*).

Toulouse and its surrounding areas are ravaged alternately by the *cers*, a west wind carrying rain clouds, and by the *autan* (*centre*).

Trees deformed by the chronic violence of the *autan* (*above*).

The Toulouse and Lauragais regions are particularly subject to alternating winds: in Occitan one talks of the weather changing to the *autan* or to the *cers*.

record falls in temperature to minus 5 or even minus 10 degrees. These contrasting conditions reveal the diversity of meteorological features of the *autan* and explain why the aspect of Midi-Pyrénées skies can vary so greatly. In fact there is no characteristic weather or sky; the direction of the wind is not always exactly the same; its strength, duration and consequences also vary. One hears references to the "*autan blanc*," or the "*autan noir*", expressions which denote a visible state of the sky. The first, the *blanc*, is characterised by very sunny weather and a blindingly luminous sky, especially on the Mediterranean side. The *autan noir* brings with it a sky heavily laden with cumulus clouds, and high clouds above them. It is this barrage of clouds which blocks the sun's rays, dulls the sky and provokes rainfall. To reduce the *autan* to these two types of sky would be to over-simplify, especially when one thinks that its territory is so vast and has such varied relief. The differences in the distance of some areas from the Mediterranean, the Pyrenees and the line of hills to the

In the 1980s, some classes from the Vincent-Auriol lycée in Revel sought to check the influence of the Pyrenees on the autan wind. Groups of balloons labelled in five languages were launched and the day, hour, weather and wind direction carefully noted. Anyone coming across a balloon was requested to send back a message with full details of its landing point. As a result, it was discovered that balloons had ended up in Cantal, in the north-east of the Massif central, at the foot of the Vosges, in the Rhine corridor and even in Czechoslovakia! In other words in an easterly or north easterly direction with regard to the launching zone. This experiment backs up the geographer, Jean-Pierre Vigneau's hypothesis according to which the autan, a wind from the eastern sector, is accompanied by an important flow from the western sector coming from over the Pyrenees. A perfectly natural phenomenon...

It is on the north side of the Montagne Noire, in the plain between Revel and Labruguière, that the most devastating squalls regularly occur.

A sounding balloon climbs up into the atmosphere in order to measure the force, speed and direction of the wind.

east and their situation on the axis of Naurouze and other large towns are factors which help to modify the characteristics of a wind susceptible to the influences of terrain.

In 1993, Arnaud Mandement, a meteorologist, published the results of his research under the title *Contribution à la connaissance du vent d'autan*. In it he notes that one cannot explain the *autan* simply by an examination of the sky. He acknowledges that the "*autan* is such a part of everyday life that it has always been judged futile to try to improve on the studies effected in the seventies." The work of Jean-Pierre Vigneau occupies a prominent place in these studies. This Toulouse geographer developed an original theory which took into account a factor neglected until then: the existence of the chain of the Pyrenees. Thus he describes a "geographical" *autan,* the strength of which is associated with a great flow of air crossing the Pyrenees from the south/south west. This theory can often be verified when the sky is cloudy: low clouds tear along in the direction of the *autan,* while higher clouds have a more perpendicular direction and seem to proceed very slowly, because of their altitude.

The result is that, whilst the air is channelled from the Aude corridor towards Toulouse, it is pressed down by the flow coming down from the north side of the Pyrenees. This double compression creates a

saucepan-lid effect, and explains the strength with which the *autan* is unleashed as it escapes from this restraint.

Early in the nineties, Météo-France, inspired by its installation on the Mirail site in Toulouse, i.e. right in the middle of *autan* territory, finally took its turn at studying the question. Analysed in its remotest details, the turbulent air revealed some of its particular features, but not all. It still retains a sufficient aura of mystery to prompt the most diverse of interpretations, supported by observations which seem to defy common sense. For instance, in Dourgne, how does the newsagent know that the east wind is going to blow the next day? Not because his rheumatism is beginning to trouble him or because the children are agitated, but because certain of his customers have asked for…bread or ham! ■

By dint of observation, dissection and analysis, the turbulent air has finally revealed some of its secrets. But it has held on to enough mysteries to allow for the most fantastical interpretations.

A wealth of

Perfect autumn stillness: a watermill on the Lot, reflected in the lazy water *(above)*.

Lake Pareloup (Tarn): water, stone and wood, as in a Japanese garden *(opposite)*.

Marc Trillard
Writer

waters

THE LOT, GERS, TARN, ARIÈGE, AVEYRON, Dordogne, Save… Rivers feed and criss-cross the lands of Midi-Pyrénées like a network of veins and arteries, weaving the land into a tight mesh of mountain springs, torrents and fountain-heads. Inevitably, the largest rivers have given their names to the *départements* they cross, since they are their sap and milk, a source of life and inspiration, feeding human activity and aspirations. For a time, they fell victims to the thoughtlessness of those who lived along their banks, polluting their waters and damaging their beds, until they realised that a lifeless river with wrecked banks is an irreparable loss. Attitudes,

Built on the banks of the Agout, these façades of Castres might almost be in Venice *(below)*.

The fishermen's huts along the Tarn, islets of great peace and beauty *(below)*.

fortunately, have changed and the waters and banks of the Garonne and the region's other rivers, whose fauna had been seriously endangered, now quiver and rustle with renewed life: spawning-grounds are once again quicksilver schools of young fry, the leafy banks throb once more with the flutter of wings and cries of birds, some of which have flown in all the way from the Atlantic. Children rediscover pleasures that their grandparents enjoyed in their own childhood, such as bathing in a bend in the river.

Even more than on the Canal du Midi, inland water transport has had its day, especially on the Garonne. Road and rail have tolled the bell of the bargee's trade for so long now that the memory of pas-

Inevitably, the largest rivers have given their names to the *départements* they cross, since they are their sap and milk, feeding human activity and aspirations.

tel, wood, cereals and wine being plied up and down the waterways has vanished. But the rivers live on, taking part in men's daily lives in countless other ways. Over and beyond evident contributions such as irrigation, which has traditionally proved so essential to farmers in our region, water has played a central part in many other activities, which would have never seen the day but for streams and rivers: those of the people who live along the Dadou, at Graulhet, or along the Arnette and Thoré, at Mazamet, who dress skins in their taweries and weave and dye goods in woollen-mills, traditions that, unfortunately, have had their heyday and may not survive long; those in Lot, at Saint-Laurent-d'Olt in Aveyron, at Viala, in Tarn, who make round-bellied earthenware and clay jars; those in Haute-Garonne, at Martres-Tolosane, who make the famous painted faience that are named after the town. All these craftsmen owe their livelihoods to the waterways they dwell by as much as to their ancestors, who handed down those precious, age-long skills. Moreover, whether it comes from the river or is collected from wells or tapped from the mains, water plays an essential part in a host of other trades that to this day are still dependent upon it.

In many places, man has owed his livelihood to water. In recent years, though, man's relationship with water has embarked on other courses, that bear no relation to work: leisure, sports and a closer interest in one's natural heritage have provided additional incentives for a close association with rivers, torrents and springs. Water has become a playmate that throbs with the thrill of excitement, a weekend and holiday rendez-vous. At Antignac, below the snow-capped Pyrenean peaks, white-water rafting provides thrills of excitement on the foaming eddies and falls of the Pique. At the opposite end of Midi-Pyrénées, on the waters of the Tarn, where it crosses the district of Albi, refurbished sailing barges offer rides that offer fewer thrills but just as many delights.

Perhaps because I was born under the sign of water, I myself have dipped into most of the watery pleasures our region offers – except those I prefer to leave to daredevils, who think nothing of hurtling down bottleneck torrents. I still remember how, as a child, standing close to my father's legs, I first saw lake Oô, at the end of what had seemed an endless climb in the Pyrenees. I felt as though I

The Canal du Midi, an artery that brings life to the villages it flows through *(above)*.

Pottery at Giroussens, in Tarn, where the traditions of glazed earthenware pots lives on to this day *(above)*.

Fishing for shad in the Garonne, near Auvillar *(top)*.

Contemplating
Lake Neouvielle,
canoeing down
the Lot, taking the
waters at Luchon:
water offers an
infinite variety of
pleasures.

had reached the world's end, a strange and indescribable land – which did not prevent my brother and me from breaking the icy peace of what had appeared to me as some sacred lake with our yells and splashing. More than once, in later years, I have dived into rivers of the Toulouse plain and the Astarac, in Gers. More than once, I have overturned in my canoe, before learning the art of rolling, as I careered

Luchon, or "the Queen of the Pyrenees". The spa's casino is a major attraction (opposite and bottom).

Barbazan, the delightfully quaint atmosphere of a grand old spa (centre).

Whatever the initial curative reason, anyone who has "taken the waters" knows what it is to feel reborn in one's body.

down the Salat, in Ariège, and the Hers-Vif, in Haute-Garonne. More recently, in Quercy, I presided over the wedding of a cousin of mine, on a large boat that sailed down the Célé river, where it flows into the Lot: the bride was beautiful, of course, the river an admiring mirror.

I was born under the sign of water, at Baden-Baden, a spa in the Black Forest, but it was not until many years later that I really got to know the world of thermal springs, and realized that they epitomized one of the great breakthroughs of civilization. Whatever the initial curative reason, anyone who has "taken the waters" knows what it is to feel reborn in one's body. In Midi-Pyrénées, we are rather fortunate in this respect. There are at least twenty spas currently operating: Ax-les-Thermes, in Ariège, Luz-Saint-Sauveur, near the National Pyrenean Park, Castéra-Verdauzan, in Armagnac, to quote just a few of those exotic-sounding names I love to hear and say. Very early on, man discovered that water could be a primary cure, the most natural medicine in the world; one spring acted on such and such a disease, another on other ailments. There is no need to list here the numerous curative properties of the thermal waters that spring up all over Midi-Pyrénées, but it is worth noting the renewed success they have enjoyed in recent years, which I see as part of a broader phenomenon, a rediscovery of one's natural environment, a return to one's "sources", back to the spring of life. ∎

Sulphurous, ferruginous or magnesian, the thermal waters of Midi-Pyrénées are rightly famed for their curative properties. Each year, more than 75 000 patients and visitors come to take the waters in the 19 spas of Midi-Pyrénées, which makes it the fourth most important thermal region in France. The spas specialise in specific ailments: Ussat-les-Bains and Bagnères-de-Bigorre for psychosomatic and neurological problems, Ax-les-Thermes, Barèges, Capvern-les-Bains, Barbotan for rheumatisms, Luchon, Barèges, Argelès-Gazost for ear-nose-and-throat illnesses. In recent years, most spas have also tried to meet growing demands for fitness and relaxation programmes. Some also open their installations to visitors on a one-day basis; thus, after a day's walking or skiing, one can take a dip in the frigidarium, caldarium or tipidarium.

GARONNE: HYMN TO A RIVER

I live very near the Garonne, in rue des Blanchers, in Toulouse, and already the street-name recalls the taweries (*blancheries*) that used to line it, thus signalling the river's proximity. The river has always been a beguiling presence, imperiously and endlessly beckoning to me, drawing me to its banks, absorbing my gaze and thoughts for hours on end. Threading through this contemplation, as I watched the river flow by, was a yearning to share with others the feelings it aroused in me. How best could I tell the river's story? Then, one day, I understood that the best thing to do was to let the Garonne tell its own story. I took a camera and went right up to its source, the Trou de Toro, and from there, followed it down again, right to its mouth, on the distant Atlantic. The end-result was a film, *Garunna, portrait of a river and its people.* The film in itself is not what matters most

> I discovered incredibly beautiful banks, islands that seemed to float suspended in time.

Born as a riotous torrent in the Val d'Aran *(far left)*, the Garonne slows and widens out, meandering below the hills of Pech David, near Toulouse *(middle left)*.

In Toulouse, the "pink city", the Bazacle dyke *(far right)*, situated between La Grave hospital and the hydroelectric plant, has a pass for upstream-migrating fish such as the shad *(middle right)*.

to me. What counts is a shared experience with a river that I learned to know intimately. Over some 600 kilometres, I came to discover unsuspected facets of the Garonne, its extraordinary liveliness, its idiosyncrasies, an infinite variety of unexpected and unique places, secrets and stories. The Garonne I discovered came alive, akin to some being that was both mythical and alive, that spoke a tongue, or myriad of tongues, through the riverside-dwellers who told me its story. I discovered incredibly beautiful banks, islands, some of which were inhabited, others not, that seemed to float suspended in time, bends in the river that embraced and sheltered unknown microcosms of fauna and flora. I got to know people who lived attuned to the river, in the intimacy of its behaviour and ways, who had learned to predict its changing moods by heeding its sounds and the colour of its waters: some were professional fishermen, others boatmen, others mere riverside-dwellers. And all those voices came together in one great hymn to the river that I can still hear, since I still live near the river and go on paying a regular tribute to its overwhelming beauty.

Sunrise over Hôtel-Dieu Saint-Jacques, Toulouse *(facing page).*

A cordillera of human activity

Patrice de Bellefon
Climber and writer

WHEN, ON A FINE DAY, ONE TRAVELS SOUTHWARDS across Midi-Pyrénées, one discovers with a sense of wonder the distant vision of our long cordillera, the Pyrenees. It unfolds across the horizon like a score of quavers and semiquavers, a wall of turrets and gateways that rises above the hills of Lauragais and Gascony, the wrinkled ridges of Plantaurel. From western Ariège to the Balaïtous mountain, on the border with Aquitaine, the Pyrenees of our region account for the highest third of the range. They include all the peaks that soar above 3,000 metres, two of which we share with Spanish Catalonia, the Pic d'Estats and Pic de Sutllo. We also share several with Aragon, where there are no less than 120 such peaks!

An exceptional viewpoint from a hilltop in Couserans, that spans at least half the chain, with legendary peaks such as Mont Valier and Pic du Midi de Bigorre clearly visible.

In the morning mist, the mountain unfolds its mysteriousness to the early walkers *(opposite)*.

With its austere north face, Vignemale (3,298 m) is one of the Pyrenean massifs that boldly asserts its high-mountain status.

Climbers who like to tackle high mountains will find in our region some of the boldest, most challenging peaks in the Pyrenees, many of them aloofly entrenched behind high-soaring rocky battlements. The north face of Vignemale (3,298 m) is a daunting architecture of blind cliffs and pillars, its robust symmetry structured by the icy features of the

Gaube pass and offering the highest limestone faces in France. Together with neighbouring Andorra, those high mountains offer some of the largest skiing areas in the Pyrenees, which are less threatened than others by the greehouse effect. Average Pyrenean summits rival in height with those of the Alps, which are indented by deep passes. The range has naturally given rise to the image of a natural barrier or wall that was dear to the Romantics. Victor Hugo saw in the Gavarnie glacier a wall that "from sea to ocean bars a continent", while Jules Michelet, the historian,

In the winter silence, the high summits cloak themselves in a snowy remoteness *(above).*

described it as "that fearsome, austere, continuous wall between Europe and Africa, between Europe and that part of Africa called Spain". Fortunately, political circumstances, European aspirations shared by people north and south of the Pyrenees, fruitful and increasingly close ties with our Catalan and Aragonese friends south of the Pyrenees, have revived the range's authentic cultural identity. Far from being a natural barrier between France and Spain, the Pyrenees are a fertile crossways of

The harshness of the higher valleys of Ariège is softened by delicate and harmonious elements in the landscape.

communities that people the valleys north and south of the range. In our region, the Pyrenees seem to illustrate all the natural and cultural idiosyncracies of the range, at every tier and level. Linguistically, Midi-Pyrénées represents six of the range's seven languages (Basque being the exception). Landscapes, of course, are extraordinarily varied, changing abruptly from one valley to the next, and often within the same valley or massif. Geologically complex massifs, where the overthrust of limestone falls pushes into dark masses of Plutonic rock that are crowned with needle-like crests, the slow erosion of the ridge by the Atlantic storms, the diversity of shapes and colours, the sheer variety of trees, all contribute to conjure up a rich anthology of rustic landscapes and arid mineral masses. Beyond the sculptures wrought by natural phenomena, the Pyrenees in our region stimulate our curiosity because of the talent with which men have shaped the landscape. All this is still visible today: valleys and mountains bear traces of a heritage shaped by a social division of property. Tracks wending up to high cols and paths leading to seasonal pastures, walled rural villages, a hint of spiritual aspirations carved in stone, all those physical and barely material traces provide a cultural dimension that underscores natural features; they are the soul and memory of the place.

Clinging to its hillside, Cominac faces the mountains of Ariège.

Traditional pens topped by haybarns, at Portet-de-Luchon.

Here, on the track leading to Balagué, time has stopped…

This wide palette of tints and moods, this rich plurality, unusually circumscribed within a relatively restricted geographical area, are a tribute to the diversity of the Pyrenees' personality, in much the same way as, on a global scale, cultural variety makes for the unity of mankind.

To the east, Ariège raises up its battlements of mountains. Its relief is a strange world of mossy ravines, dripping slopes, stray waterfalls, rocky ledges and overhanging firns. The same is true even of its highest peaks, such as Mont Valier, which shelters the easternmost residual glacier of the Pyrenees. The most outstanding sites of the higher Ariège mountains, which used to be magnificently wild, have been tamed and harnessed to provide settings for leisure activities. In contrast, one rediscovers the preserved soul of a remoter Ariège in isolated massifs where nature is its own reward, up southbound routes that follow patient, silent tracks along slopes where an exuberant vegetation reaches out to the Mediterranean

Resting in his hut: shepherds are the keepers of the Pyrenean soul *(below).*

Cirès, overlooked by its church: a village in the Oueil valley *(below right).*

warmth while still fanned by Atlantic breezes. Steep mountain slopes roll scattered boulders down into kitchen-gardens that cling to its lower slopes, on the outskirts of compact villages where poignantly rustic walls house a frugal yet incredibly tender domesticity.

When exploring the Ariège and Couserans valleys and massifs, one must not overlook the delights of the Volp and Plantaurel hills and ridges. In my opinion they are the most domestic and harmonious Pyrenean foothills in the whole of Midi-Pyrénées. Rural landscapes

stretch along the lazy slopes of what are in fact the range's last folds and tremors, facing the regal panorama of its most elevated crags. Landscapes are harmoniously laid out, in a geometric patchwork of woodland and pasture-land that respects unpredictable contours and encloses lovely hamlets which nestle deep in the greenery.

The Val d'Aran, where Gascon is the official language, cuts deeply in between the mountains of Couserans and Comminges, before coming to an abrupt end to the south-west, just below the Maladeta massif, where Pic d'Aneto (3,404 m) soars up, the highest peak in the whole of the

Pyrenees. The whole central part of the range rises up and broadens out here, giving way, at the level of Luchon, to two parallel alignments of peaks, most of which are more than 3,000 metres high. To the south, the Maladeta massif, and to the north, this side of the Venasque valley, the Posets massif (3,371 m), which is the second highest in the Pyrenees. This is the heartland of the highest mountains in Midi-Pyrénées, a world that matches contemporary aspirations and where, over the past two centuries, we have learned that verticality is part and parcel of our physical and aesthetic sensibility. This part of the Pyrenees is a kind of sanctuary, an instance of "intrepid geography", that attracts those who are fascinated by high-mountain climbing and trekking.

Strange though it may seem, this seemingly continuous line of high mountains, that provokes great climactic contrasts between north

Poignantly rustic walls house a frugal yet incredibly tender domesticity.

The skiing resort at Superbagnères lights up the snow-capped peaks.

Flowers, moorland and forests cloak the mountain slopes. Herbalism is a favourite hobby in the Pyrenees.

Sheep-grazing, one of the highlights of pastoral life in the Pyrenees.

and south, has brought about some of the most fruitful and lasting exchanges between the communities living on either side of the range. The higher Luchon valley used to communicate relatively easily with the Val d'Aran through the Portillon pass and the summer pastures of Campsaur that, to the east, overlook the site of Hospice de France: those pastures are still shared by the shepherds of Val d'Aran and Luchon valley. In spite of the difficulties they had to overcome to reach and pass Port de la Glère (2,367 m), travellers traditionally took that route and cultivated close ties with the inhabitants of Venasque and distant Aragon, which attracted merchants from Toulouse and Auvergne – until, some time in the 16th century, a pass was cleared with shovels and pickaxes at the Venasque col (2,444 m), which was henceforth opened up to mules and horses. After a long walk in a magnificent setting, this narrow breach in the austere, rocky rampart rewards hikers with the most majestic view

Port de la Canau, between two rocky pyramids, at the western end of the Troumouse cirque, was a traditional route towards the Bielsa valley, in Aragon.

Illustration by Jouas.
At each step, the man in
the picture risks being
swallowed by the crevices
of the Vignemale glacier
(below).

The waterfall at the
cirque de Gavarnie,
one of the site's many
attractions. Illustration
by Viollet-le-Duc *(bottom)*.

of the Maladeta massif. The whole area, reaching from Pic de Campsaur to the east, to Pic Sacroux, which, to the west, frowns over the Glère pass, is one of the most significant "cultural landscapes" in the whole range.

The town council of Luchon has wisely undertaken to restore Hospice de France, an ancient and famous hospice – as its name suggests – that already existed in the Middle Ages, situated at an important junction, where Val d'Aran, Comminges and Aragon meet, a historic, pastoral, traditional crossways, where popular folklore has blended battles linked to the conflicts that used to oppose France and Spain and secret feats involving local clans. It is to be hoped that the project goes ahead. One of the ways in which the valleys of the Pyrenees can hope to get the best out of their heritage without wrecking it irrecoverably is to offer sites that combine the pleasures of historical reminiscence and geographical exoticism, while being located in different areas, instead of being concentrated in just a few places.

At the far end of Comminges, beyond Pics Belloc and Gourgs Blancs, where the region advances into the *département* of Midi-Pyrénées, the range leaves behind the more mineral, vigorous traits of its higher reaches. Here, the inhospitable peaks recall, albeit with fewer natural eccentricities, the changeable mood and style of the Ariège peaks.

Aragnouet, a village nestling at the bottom of the Aure valley, is fortunate enough to own and control a wide mountainous area that includes the impressive rock faces of Barroude, the easternmost edge of the Mont-Perdu National Park, and the finest of the countless lakes that dot the massif of Pics Long et Néouvielle. Rather like the Encantats in the Val d'Aran, this granitic region offers a stimulating and delightfully contrasted landscape of sheer peaks and slender needles, that are mirrored in the lazy waters of countless lakes that glimmer like intensely tinted gems set in pleasant hollows. The tiny medieval chapel of Aragnouet, that used to belong to a now-vanished hospice, reminds us of the passes that used to lead towards the Aragonese valley of Bielsa, towards Gèdre and Gavarnie to the west, through the Campbieil pass, or the sanctuary of Héas, along a tricky route that followed the narrow Aiguillous ridge.

Here we are, at the heart of the Mont-Perdu massif, a site consecrated by Unesco which Midi-Pyrénées jointly controls with Aragon. The overall natural features are marked by a geological unity due to massive overthrusts of limestone. At the heart of this massif rises Mont Perdu (3,353 m): to the north, it orchestrates the ample majesty of the Troumouse, Estaubé and Gavarnie cirques, with their cold abysses, and to the south, on the Aragonese side, the parched harshness of karst peaks

La Chapelle de N.-D. de Héas
après l'avalanche du 23 Janvier 1915

A party of walkers
follows the guide up the
Portillon; by Jouas *(top)*.

Notre-Dame de Héas:
the chapel was a
sanctuary, which also
included a hospice,
where travellers stopped
to worship Our Lady of
the Snow *(above)*.

and sweeping reaches of high-mountain pastures deeply indented by the extraordinary canyons of Pineta, Añisclo and Ordesa. Over some twenty kilometres, the line of peaks, which average 3,000 m, makes for sharp climactic contrasts and explains the exceptional diversity of a rich endemic vegetation and fauna. These climactic and geo-morphological contrasts contributed to shape human activity, and resulted in a variety of crops, produce and resources that differed between the communities of the north and south sides of the range and ensured a mutual dependence, a historic culture of land-swapping, of exchange and barter, of manifold ties and hence, an attachment to peaceable relations.

"Lies i patzarias", ties and peace, between the Aure, Barèges, Bielsa and Broto valleys take us back to the concept of cultural landscapes. In other countries, communities living on either side of mountain ranges have worked out such relationships too; yet around the massif of Tres

Pic de Marboré, overlooking the regal amphitheatre of the cirque de Gavarnie.

Mont Perdu orchestrates the ample majesty of the Troumouse, Estaubé and Gavarnie cirques, with their cold abysses.

Serols-Mont Perdu, the communities too, as well as the site, would deserve to be consecrated by Unesco, since they have evolved into a sophisticated collection of ties that apply to pastoral rights, to the free movement of people and goods, to mutual neutrality in case of conflict: evolved very early on, they are a survival of an old heritage of shared customs.

In the first decades of the Christian era, the nomadic graziers who had been ranging over the massif for 15,000 or 20,000 years settled into a sedentary life. Very early on, they organised exchanges between the northern and southern communities. In the Middle Ages, the kings of Aragon called upon the inhabitants of the northern side to help them protect their subjects against Muslim invaders. Relations multiplied, with the higher passes seeing more and more travellers go by. The mountain communities' bravery was rewarded with extensive franchises and a greater degree of independence. Henceforth, treaties of "lies i patzarias" were drawn up by their elected representatives, who were chosen among the heads of households. With time, the expansion of trade was also covered by additional clauses that guaranteed the free movement of goods and people and provided for compensation in the case of travellers being the victims of community feuds or fights. Over the centuries, these treaties were improved upon and several times, up to the French revolution, the neutrality of the valleys of Mont-Perdu was confirmed,

despite the wars that opposed the kingdoms of France and Spain, and even inspired similar agreements between other valleys along the range.

To this day, as a legacy of those antique agreements, the pasturelands of the Ossoue valley, on the territory of the village of Gavarnie, are indivisibly owned by the people of the Barèges valley and the Aragonese graziers who cross the Bernatoire col every year, leading their herds of cows to the fresher, greener grassland on the northern side of the mountain. This history and legacy of a wonderful alliance, this

A legend spectacularly written in stone, Roland's Breach was also a passageway for secret exchanges between the communities north and south of the mountain.

The astronomers' observatory of Pic du Midi de Bigorre, under the snow: it commands a superb skyline.

The village of Gerde and Campan valley, where the mountains slope gently down to the plain.

intimate symbiosis of man and his mountain environment, invite us to read the cultural and social cohesion of a world that was until recently presented as an admirable succession of cirques and canyons, with no regard for their human dimension.

The discovery of cultural idiosyncrasies in a context of natural diversity is what increasingly attracts visitors to the area, hence the need to preserve a range of economic activities that ensure the survival of the human facets of these beautiful landscapes. The notion of "cultural landscapes" is particularly appropriate in the case of the Pyrenees. Beyond the immediate economic and environmental impact, one can

sense the benefits that beautiful valleys such as Campan and Arras would draw from being promoted to the status of a consecrated site, like Mont-Perdu. Few places indeed blend the delights of mountain scenery and homely rusticity with such welcoming grace.

The purpose of being classed as a protected site is not merely to ensure the survival of an exceptional ensemble, but to offer a model where past traditions and present-day human activity blend and look towards the future. Local harmony based on a native authenticity, on a genuine identity and way of life intimately rooted in an aesthetic setting, is the best possible way of preserving a unique heritage that can only attract a mutually enriching type of tourism. ■

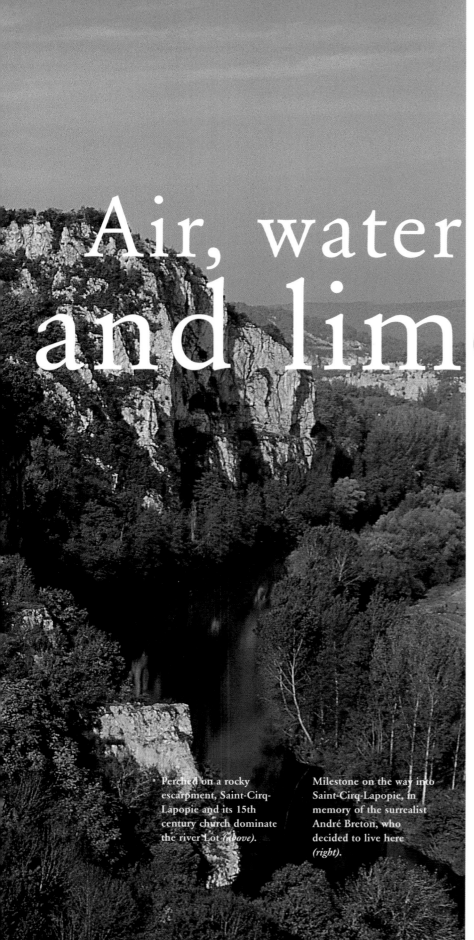

Pierre Le Coz
Writer

Air, water and limestone

CLINGING ONTO THE FLANKS OF THE ROCKY CLIFFS which tower over the river Lot, the village of Saint-Cirq-Lapopie always gives visitors the impression of being about to slide lock, stock and barrel into the abyss, with its church, its old houses, its flowers and inhabitants. When André Breton came across the town in 1950 he fell in love with it, so much so that he made up his mind to end his days there.

> "Saint-Cirq has simply woven its enchantment in me and rooted me here forever. I have ceased to feel the desire to be elsewhere."

What exactly is the nature of this enchantment, which should make this surrealist poet, an adept of urban life and a

Perched on a rocky escarpment, Saint-Cirq-Lapopie and its 15th century church dominate the river Lot *(above)*.

Milestone on the way into Saint-Cirq-Lapopie, in memory of the surrealist André Breton, who decided to live here *(right)*.

Luzech, a peninsula
between the arms of the
Lot *(below)*.

It has sometimes been
necessary to bore through
solid rock in order for
cars to pass *(below right)*.

seasoned traveller, decide to settle in a tiny village somewhere in the upper Lot valley? Maybe it is that the village of Saint-Cirq itself seems ever ready for the off: tethered only to the clouds, the village has just to slide down the hill and abandon itself to the river's flow to begin a long migration. Certain landscapes hold us spellbound by their essentially earthy dimension; here, it is rather the aerial aspect of the countryside which wins us over: the grey or green swell of the rolling hills under that other swell, this time of the sky; the hew of an axe wielded by the river Lot into soft limestone which creaks in places like old roofing; the gaping abysses of Padirac and Lacave, which both terrify and delight walkers. Suspension, stupefaction, vertigo: paradoxically, it is

these traits which makes it tempting to "anchor" oneself here: wistful longings for far-off places, vague desires for another life on the slow side of the clouds are shouldered by the landscape which bears the weight of the sweet melancholy and regret of its inhabitants…

Between Capdenac and Vers, the road follows the course of the Lot, sometimes caught between the river and the ochre or grey precipices, sometimes climbing up the latter for a glimpse of the surrounding countryside. In summer, there is a striking contrast between the arid landscape of the *causses*, bared to the scorching Occitanian sun, and the luxurious green foliage of the vegetation down below. The narrow canyon of the Lot appears like a slash of freshness in the midst of an incandescent limestone desert. Then, dipping down once again, the path plunges into the deep gorges – where it has sometimes been necessary, in order for cars to pass, to bore through solid rock – before emerging into more airy parts of valley. From high up in the Saint-Cirq escarpment, looking out towards the west, this fairy-tale succession of towering precipices and wells of greenery, mysterious and maternal, within which the Lot coils, seems to lay bare the very sex of the earth. And suddenly we feel we would like to live serenely under this changing sky, to set down our luggage once and for all like the author of *Signe ascendant*. Or else, on the contrary, we dream of becoming a pilgrim marching towards some holy place, Conques or Compostela, tramping in the direction of the setting sun, anxious to find refuge before nightfall. And so we climb back into the car and drive down the

Cahors resembles nothing so much as a Tuscan town which has drifted its way westwards to bump up against this almost perfect coil of the river.

slope away from Saint-Cirq. Twenty minutes later, we are in Cahors, the ancient capital of Quercy.

Cahors, a walled town snuggling in a loop of the Lot, has more than a hint of Italy in its pink roofs, its towers and steeples, its marriage of stone and brick, as if some Tuscan town has drifted westwards to bump up against this almost perfect coil of the river. In the Middle Ages, the town went through a period of prosperity, thanks to its Lombard bankers: at this time its banking customers comprised the royal families of all Europe and the city was one of the most flourishing of the kingdom. A feeling of opulence and easy living has remained, despite the vagaries of history, which serves to emphasise the austerity of the surrounding *causses*. "Cahors, a gentle town in the form of a teardrop", was how Denis Tillinac, the novelist, put it. Try

The Valentré bridge in Cahors and its three square towers remember the bitter struggle with the English in the Middle Ages *(above)*.

Léon Gambetta, born in Cahors in 1838, was an illustrious partisan of the Republic. A statue pays homage to him in the capital of Lot *(opposite)*.

ambling through the maze of mediaeval streets and wandering along the green and shady banks of the Lot, then climb to the top of Saint-Cyr to look out over the town and surrounding hills. From this angle, the city is a mass of interlocking tiles from which emanates a murmur of ancient times and trades. Further towards the north can be seen the foothills of the *causse* of Gramat then, downstream, past the arches of the famous Valentré bridge, the "land of meanders". Standing before it, like a sentinel on its rocky escarpment, is the tower of the Château de Mercuès.

The former residence of the bishop-earls of Cahors, the castle is now a hotel. From its windows is a vertiginous drop of a hundred metres to the waters of the river below. After Saint-Cirq-Lapopie and Mont Saint-Cyr, here is another chasm where one's gaze is drawn into the abyss or far across towards the distant west, in the direction of Luzech and Puy-l'Évêque. It was here that in bygone times, before the irruption of the railroad, convoys of flat-bottomed boats called *gabares* transporting wine and wood – the riches and work of a whole area – would glide along on their way to Bordeaux and the ocean. A popular saying had it that "sailors would bed down twice at Luzech" and indeed, it is true that the boatmen would start off in the early morning and take the whole day to circumnavigate this loop of the river, so that in the evening they would be… back where they had started! A dangerous undertaking it was too, to sail around Luzech. A strong, sometimes uncontrollable current drove the boats towards the rocks – including the famous Roc de Perdigal – and caused a great many shipwrecks.

A sanctuary to this half-legend, Notre-Dame-de-l'Île, also known as Notre-Dame des Mariniers, is still standing, a modest chapel at the end of the loop encircled by the precipitous slopes of the opposite bank. A commemorative plaque that was set there by pious mariners to thank the Virgin for some miraculous rescue is still visible. At this place, the walker is struck by the contrast between the two banks: the one flat, low, with cultivated land, on which Notre-Dame was built, the other wild with sheer cliffs which compel the river to turn back on itself. It is as though the impetuous Lot, fresh from the mountains, has tried to force its way through to the south and that only the mineral

A bunch of *auxerrois*, otherwise known as *côt*, grapes, the star vine of Cahors wines *(above)*.

Lot limestone. Both landscape and traditional buildings carry its imprint *(opposite)*.

Half-timbered houses in Figeac with shutters painted in the blue typical of Quercy *(below)*.

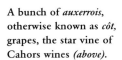

Circumnavigating Luzech was a perilous undertaking; a violent, sometimes irresistible current drove boats towards the rocks and destroyed a good many.

The chapel of Notre-Dame-de-l'Île in Luzech contains numerous votive offerings left there by mariners descending the Lot. The loop-shaped garden is a patchwork of green and brown.

In the setting sun, the entire town of Puy-l'Évêque, with its old houses, castle and parks, admires itself in the now peaceful waters of the Lot.

barrier of these austere hills has prevented it. It is this very combat between water and rock that gave birth to the astonishing Lot valley, which carves its way through the limestone, caught between desire and necessity.

At Puy-L'Évêque, it is once again the whole town – its old houses, towers, *donjon* and parks – that is tumbling down the hill before coming to a halt at the river-side. The surrounding country is greener though, more cheery than the austere region of Saint-Cirq-Lapopie. This is the land of the Cahors vineyards. Once renowned, they were devastated by the phylloxera outbreak but have now definitively regained their reputation. The wine, a dark ruby red, is the slow-

This *cazelle* or *gariote* used to serve as a shelter for shepherds or beasts.

The Place des Écritures, which announces the entrance of the Champollion museum at Figeac, is a huge, faithful reproduction of the Rosetta stone.

Mercuès Castle, the favourite residence of the bishops of Cahors in the 13th century, is now a high class hotel.

The Cahors wine, a dark ruby red, is the slowest, most meditative fruit of the Lot valley.

est, most meditative fruit of the valley. From the first sip, one recognises its marvellous paradox: at once delicate and deep, tart but with a feminine languor, the product of an unruly land which dreams of embracing the sky, of rising to meet the sun. It is the convergence in one brew of the seasons in which it was born, sprouted and matured – the warmth of the hills in summer; the harshness of the winter mists and ice –, the expression of this land caught between the river and the clouds. ■

A native of Figeac, Jean-François Champollion became one of the greatest Egyptologists of the 19th century. His fame is inextricably linked with hieroglyphs as he was the first to have deciphered this strange writing, composed of pictures many believed to be simple decorative drawings. Some of the texts he had at his disposal for this accomplishment were discovered during Bonaparte's campaign in Egypt. One of them was particularly precious, a text engraved on a stone in hieroglyphs, accompanied by a Greek translation, which was found near to the town of Rosetta in the Nile delta. After ten years of solid work, he succeeded in solving the mystery. He was successively curator in the Egyptology section of the Louvre, then teacher at the Collège de France, and is also the author of an Egyptian grammar book and dictionary.

Paths

of ambition

Inventing
the sky

François Besse & Gil Roy
Journalists

"**T**HERE CAN BE NO PILOT WITHOUT A TEAM; the higher and faster we fly, the more we need a chain of highly skilled professionals, bonded together by unfailing trust in each other". Make no mistake, the man who pronounced this phrase had absolutely nothing of those chilly technocrats who avoid "human factors" like the plague. Bernard Ziegler is unquestionably in the ranks of those who can say "I was there". This born pilot – he was both fighter pilot and test pilot –, who was a member of the crew who flew the first A-300 in 1972, simply understood that great ventures such as that of aeronautics in Midi-Pyrénées, and more specifically Airbus, cannot be the work of one man.

The nose of an Airbus jumbo jet, one of the symbols of the aeronautics boom in Midi-Pyrénées and Europe *(above)*.

The pilot Marcel Doret, many times holder of the world record for speed and a close friend of Dewoitine, standing in front of a D-1 *(bottom left)*.

Pierre-Georges Latécoère, born in 1883 in Bagnères-de-Bigorre, threw himself into aeronautics and set up Lignes Latécoère in 1919 *(bottom right)*.

You will never catch such a man talking of heroism, bragging about "conquering the sky", at Blagnac or anywhere else, and yet when your eyes cross, these lines from the first chapter of Courrier Sud, printed on the yellowed pages of the Nouvelle Revue Française, will come into your mind: *"Mail France-America left Toulouse 05.45 stop passed Alicante 11.10. Toulouse was talking. Toulouse, start of the line. God far away."* Saint-Exupéry's writings spawned a whole mythology, along with men such as Daurat, Mermoz, Guillaumet... Whose heart, in Midi-Pyrénées or elsewhere, has not throbbed and trembled to the rhythm of this era, this "sky western" whose camp was established in the old aerodrome of Montaudran, where the Latécoère and Aéropostale airlines, forefathers to our modern industry and airlines, took to the air?

And yet in the 1930s, as our intrepid leather-clad heroes were heading off for Saint-Louis-du-Sénégal or Buenos Aires, aeronautical history was already 40 years old. It all began on the 9th October 1890. That day, for the first time in the human history, a man was to take off behind the controls of a strange spluttering machine of his own construction. This man was Clément Ader, a native of Muret, in Haute-Garonne. With a few bounds of the *Éole* he had invented aviation. Others were to follow in his footsteps and write some of the most prestigious chapters of world aeronautics. From the Wright brother's Flyer to the Airbus A-340-600 quadrijet, from the Morane-Saulnier single-engine aircraft to the supersonic Concorde – the most prestigious of all aircraft to have taken off in the sky of Occitania –, Midi-Pyrénées has been a hotbed of creativity and daring since the very origins of aviation. For here in Midi-Pyrénées, the conquest of the sky is first and foremost the story of men who dared...

Émile Dewoitine and Marcel Doret pictured in front of a D-27 in 1928 *(top)*.

Clément Ader's n°3 aircraft, successor to the historic *Éole*, which was presented notably at the Universal Exhibition of 1900 *(centre)*.

A flashback to a heroic era; this postcard was sent by Émile Dewoitine to his mother *(opposite)*.

In 1912, two Frenchmen, Léon Morane and Maurice Saulnier, launched themselves into the design and construction of aeroplanes. It was on board one of their planes, the Morane H, in 1913, that Roland Garros became the first to cross the Mediterranean sea. Their first successful venture was the fighter MS-AI employed in squadrons during the first world war. Between the wars, they consolidated their reputation with a series of student planes such as the Parasol which were used in the training centres of the French air force to train thousands of civil and military pilots. The famous Étampes patrol, an ancestor of the *Patrouille de France*, flew MS-225s.

These two images are separated by 70 years: one of the *Lignes Latécoère* aircraft *(above)* and an Airbus A-320 *(below)*.

The arrival
in Toulouse of
Caravelle *(top left)*.
Blagnac airport
(top right).
The making
of Concorde
*(bottom left and
right)*.

CONCORDE N° 11

For their part, Latécoère, Daurat, Mermoz, Guillaumet and Saint-Exupéry entered into the legend of Aéropostale on board Breguet and Latécoère aircraft loaded down with mail sacks. They would take off in the early morning from the Montaudran airfield. Some years later, Émile Dewoitine was to propose his Dewoitine D-520 to the French military aviation authorities; along with the MS-406, it would constitute the backbone of the French fighter aircraft fleet in 1940.

And yet, although Midi-Pyrénées, especially Toulouse, is now inseparably linked with aeronautics, the "*Ville rose*" could all too easily have missed its vocation. Customs change with the times: in 1781, for instance, the Montgolfier brothers were refused authorisation to fly over the town by parliament, on the basis that "curiosity could distract the faithful from accomplishing acts of religion". An infuriating setback, but a mistake that Toulouse would do its best never to repeat. Its opportunity came with the first world war and the syndrome of 1870. Far removed from the front, Toulouse was an ideal aeronautics base. Émile Dewoitine was looking for a site on which to build an enormous manufacturing workshop: he found it to the north of the Minimes area. This was the beginning of the Saint-Éloi factories, the precursor of the industrial complex of Aerospatiale, now situated near Blagnac airport.

With 1945 and the end of hostilities came the chapter of civil air transport. In Toulouse, engineers were to concentrate on the new generation of commercial aircraft represented by the Caravelle. In Tarbes, on the Ossun aerodrome, Morane-Saulnier developed a range of light aircraft, for military and civil use, with its Rallye family of single-engine planes. This model, capable of taking off and landing on small airfields, prefigures the current range of aircraft from Socata (a firm manufacturing aircraft for tourism and business purposes, the general aviation branch of the Aerospatiale group, now EADS), which took over from Morane-Saulnier. The design and production of light aircraft nowadays represents less than a half of the workload of Socata, which has become more of an industrial subcontractor for the large aeronautics programmes, delivering structural elements to the likes of Eurocopter, Dassault Aviation, the American Lockheed-Martin and also its parent company, Airbus. Socata belongs to a group of firms in the Midi-Pyrénées region working for the major European and American aeronautics and space companies. By combining their skill and reactivity, they have contributed to the fantastic success of Airbus, now the second largest manufacturer of commercial aircraft in the

A heady sight: the streamlined design of this A-330 *(opposite)*.

Pierre Baud, former head of flight testing at Airbus Industrie, and a crew running texts on an A-310 *(below)*.

Airbus had to make a considerable effort in order to counter Boeing's supremacy and win its share of international markets.

world. Only thirty years were needed for the latter to set themselves on an equal footing with Boeing, an extraordinary feat considering the hold the giant from Seattle had on the world commercial aircraft market and the quality of its products.

It was an exploit few believed would come off in the mid-sixties when the idea of collaborating on the building of a European wide-body aircraft was aired, and the project would undoubtedly have stayed on the drawing board if it had not been for the determination of a handful of people. This is characteristic of Airbus history: at each crucial stage in its development it has been able to count on committed and strong-minded people to overcome the inevitable obstacles. This is how such an eminently industrial era came to acquire the flavour of a saga…

The first of these individuals was unquestionably Roger Béteille, then Technical Director at Sud-Aviation, who embarked on a secret study for the A-300 at a time when the French, German and British had given up the idea in favour of other, more promising lines of development such as Mercure, BAC-1.11 and above all, Concorde. In his "clandestine" design offices, a small group of engineers and technicians worked on the draft of a 23-seater medium-haul aircraft, a precursor of the Airbus.

Meanwhile, Henri Ziegler, an Engineer General for aviation, was appointed head of Sud-Aviation, charged with reviving the Concorde project. He had been speaking out in favour of the creation of a European aeronautics consortium since the end of the war and agreed to see through the supersonic programme on condition that he was given authorisation to save the Airbus project. Roger Béteille could thus come out into the open in 1968. A decision to reject the new Rolls-Royce engine led to the British pulling out of the programme. Airbus was thus set up by France and Germany and on 28th October 1972, the A-300B1 lined up on the runway of Toulouse-Blagnac airport for the first ever flight of an Airbus. In 1999, the threshold of 2,000 deliveries was crossed.

Airbus's commercial success stems above all from its capacity for innovation. The concept of jet engines placed at the rear of the Caravelle fuselage was the reason behind the success of the twin-engines of regional transport, and no aircraft in the world, civil or military, has equalled Concorde's performance of maintaining supersonic flight for several hours… The know-how acquired by the Toulouse design offices has always been put to good use. The A-310 was the first to make use of cathode ray tube display and the twin piloting which

Bernard Ziegler and his crew are cheered as they arrive at Blagnac runway on 25th October 1991. They have just successfully concluded the first flight of the A-340, the Airbus long-haul aircraft *(above)*.

The tail of an ATR 72-500 *(opposite)*.

ATR is a joint French and Italian project for regional transport aircraft launched in equal (50/50) partnership in 1981 by two leading European aeronautics manufacturers, Aerospatiale, now EADS, and Aeritalia, now Alenia/Aerospazio of the Finmeccanica group.
The ATR 42's maiden flight took place in August 1984, followed by the ATR 72 in 1989. The ATR 42-500 and ATR 72-500, the new generation of ATR-500s, which came into service in 1995, are ideal over short distances and reputed for their reliability, their cost effectiveness and their high level of comfort. ATR is now the leading manufacturer of turboprops in the 40- to 70-seater market with more than 630 aircraft delivered to over a hundred customers spread over all continents. The group was reinforced in June 2001 by the merging of industrial activities which until then had been shared between the two partners, along with the commercial activities of the group; only the fuselage and wings are now manufactured in the Alenia and EADS factories. ATR has subsidiaries in Washington and Singapore.

An incredible impression of power is given off by the enormous jet engines of the A-330, one of the Airbus range of widebodies.

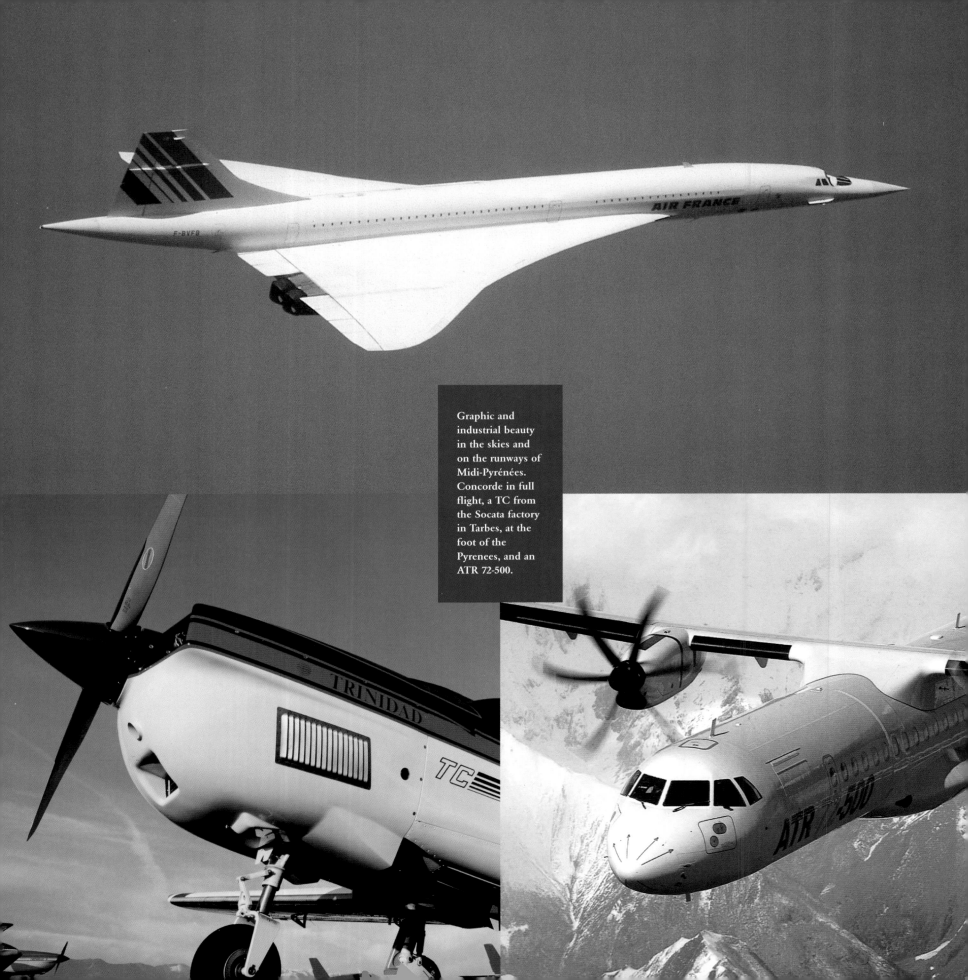

Graphic and industrial beauty in the skies and on the runways of Midi-Pyrénées. Concorde in full flight, a TC from the Socata factory in Tarbes, at the foot of the Pyrenees, and an ATR 72-500.

was to revolutionise air transport. Six years later, the A-320 ushered in the era of electric controls and computer assisted piloting. Another strong point in Airbus's strategy was the concept of families of aircraft. Ever since the A-310, Airbus has offered airlines a homogeneous range with which to optimise their fleet. Airbus invented the concept of "communality" in which planes of different types shared enough points in common for their maintenance and operation to be common as well. For crews this meant that with a minimum of training they could switch from an A-330 twin jet to an A-340 quadrijet. The heterogeneous nature of Boeing's range excludes these easy switches which allow airlines to cut costs significantly.

Despite these trump cards, Airbus had to make a considerable effort in order to counter Boeing's supremacy and win its share of international markets and, once again, it is a few individuals who have succeeded in tipping the balance. It is astonishing to note how such top civil servants as Bernard Lathière or Jean Pierson – nicknamed the bear of the Pyrénées –, who were appointed to the head of the group by political bodies, were willing to act as glorified sales reps in order to force decisive contracts. They never hesitated to take a personal stand in order to turn a decision in Airbus's favour. Noël Forgeard, the fourth head in Airbus's history, personally visited all airlines liable to add a super jumbo-jet to their fleet, so as to secure sufficient purchase orders to convince the consortium's shareholders in 2000 to go ahead with the programme A-3XX, now known as the A-380. And plenty of other projects are still in the pipeline for years to come, such as a worthy successor to Concorde…

Heads of industry or brilliant inventors, it is their passion that drives them to add their chapter to the history of aviation in Midi-Pyrénées.

We could be forgiven for thinking we'd just taken a leap into the future on discovering this computer-generated image of the forthcoming A-380, an enormous aircraft combining state-of-the-art technology and respect for the environment *(above)*.

Whether major industrial bosses or brilliant inventors, all those who have helped write the story of aviation in Midi-Pyrénées and who, as each day passes, are adding new pages to this fantastic saga of the skies, share the same passion. And it is this very passion that is the driving force behind students and research scientists from the "*grandes écoles*" and laboratories implanted in Toulouse, who are preparing to play their part in this prestigious heritage. At Blagnac, Airbus crews, busy training in flight simulators, are the direct descendants of the student pilots from the first flying school in the world, set up at the foot of the Pyrenees by the Wright brothers as far back as 1908… ■

The cockpit consoles of the different Airbuses are more or less identical. Pilots can thus switch from one plane to another after a very short training period *(opposite)*.

Midi-

Pyrénées seen from space

Christophe Chaffardon
Scientific mediator
Head of projects at the Cité
de l'espace

SO MUCH MORE THAN A TERRITORY, this word which sets our childish imaginations free and enables us to transcend our human condition. Space. The original place of creation which crystallises humanity's hopes, fears and questionings. In the beginning humanity had no more than the twinkling of stars, mute white lights, with which to feed its thirst for answers, an astral ballet it had to decipher, century after century, and which it continues to decipher, untiringly.

Then history opened the door on the most extraordinary voyages. Thanks to the invention of the wheel, the fuselage and the propeller, and then jet propulsion, space travel became possible. Vertical flights beyond the sea of clouds, towards the black, empty and infinite sky that is space.

Techniques advanced at a staggering pace. In the space of a few decades in the 20th century, the era of pioneers gave way to an era in which space represented a vital economic activity spawning the most varied applications.

A fascinating image of the Earth as seen from space, taken from the Russian space station *Mir.*

In the offices of Alcatel Space, one of the most dynamic firms in this sector *(opposite).*

The antagonism between Americans and Soviets was the initial driving force behind this evolution. It was a desire for conquest which led to the very first exploits: on the Soviet side, the first satellite in orbit around the Earth – Sputnik, on 4th October 1957 – then the first man aboard a satellite – Youri Gagarine, on 12th April 1963. Later on, the first man – American – to walk on the moon, on 21st July 1969. France entered this race to the stars in 1959 and opened a specialised centre for

After more than three million years of existence, humankind can at last admire the breathtaking beauty of this blue planet and, by getting to understand it, can better protect it.

Interferometric image of the largest Martian volcano observed to date, Olympus-Mons *(above)*.

Space research is propelled by ever more complicated mathematical calculations *(opposite)*.

study two years later on 18th December 1963. This is how the CNES (National centre for space studies) was born, charged with setting up a space policy to match the scope of French ambitions. Taking advantage of a plan to decentralise engineering colleges specialising in aeronautics and space studies, the CNES rapidly moved part of its activities from Paris to Toulouse, and work started on the Lespinet complex in 1966. After all, there was no reason why the Toulouse of the skies shouldn't blast through a thin layer of atmosphere!

More arrivals were to follow as research laboratories and other high-tech industries converted to spatial activities, choosing for the main part to set up in the area around the CST (Toulouse space centre) at Lespinet. The "*Ville rose*" was thus gradually to become the capital of European space co-operation, a fact which is magnificently illustrated by each new launch of an *Ariane* rocket, whose operations are monitored as closely from Toulouse as from Kourou. At the present time, more than nine thousand people are involved in space activities in the region, approximately a half of the total workforce for this sector in France.

The comet Hale-Bopp crossing the skies of the Pyrenees over the Pic du Midi observatory in Bigorre *(opposite).*

Like a sentinel of the skies perched at an altitude of 2,877 metres, the Pic du Midi observatory has been an exceptional observational tool ever since 1882. Initially a weather station, the site enjoys ideal conditions for gazing into the universe: luminosity almost nil, a clear atmosphere and low turbulence. It was from this station in the sixties that a team of British astronomers took thousands of photographs of the moon in order to prepare for the Apollo landings... As well as carrying out research work on solar physics, planetology and the study of atmospheric ozone, the site was recently opened up to tourists to fulfil ordinary mortals' dreams of being pioneers of astronomy – at least for the space of a few hours.

These regional players have recognised the vast potential of this area, developing a comprehensive range of contemporary space applications.

Take earth observation, for instance. At last, after more than three million years of existence, humankind can at last take a step back from this terrestrial space craft of ours and take a look at the beauty of our blue planet. The images of *Topex-Poseidon*, and *Jason*, its successor – a joint French and American project in which the CNES and Alcatel Space contributed the impressive on board instruments – give us crucial information on the world's oceans. CLS Argos, a firm based in Ramonville-Saint-Agne, sifts this precious data and diffuses it to a global community of oceanographers, climatologists and other impatient scientists. Their neighbour, Spot-Image, distributes observations of the earth coming from the Spot satellites, a fruit of the CNES's collaboration with its industrial partners in Toulouse, the two largest manufacturers of satellites in Europe, Matra Marconi Space, now Astrium, and Alcatel Space. Now famous world-wide, these images are an irreplaceable source of information in numerous areas: agriculture,

A satellite placed in orbit carries out its role as messenger: television, telephony and the Internet.

geology, cartography, oil and mineral prospecting, the monitoring of natural catastrophes, the environment, risk management… the list is endless. And who better to forecast the vagaries of the weather than Météo-France, based in Saint-Simon, with the help of images emanating from the European

meteorological lookout, *Meteosat*! Space also signifies communication: space relays are already old news, and competition is stiff on favourite

The Night of the stars, in midsummer, in the Gers town of Fleurance, enables amateur astronomers to explore the constellations *(left)*.

Under the protection of their big brother at Bigorre, several regional observatories offer initiation courses in space discovery. With the aid of simple binoculars or powerful telescopes, the stars are persuaded to yield some of their secrets at such observatories as Jolimont, in the heights of Toulouse, the Pleiades in Rieux Volvestre, also in Haute-Garonne, the Ferme des étoiles at Fleurance in Gers, Montredon-Labessonié in Tarn or Sabarat in Ariège.

orbits – those at 36,000 kilometres from the earth's equator, where an orbiting satellite will stay permanently opposite the same point on the globe, carrying out impeccably its role as messenger and relaying a variety of information from television to telephony and the Internet. The extraordinary – and growing – market for space telecommunications leaves no-one indifferent: month after month, the order books of Alcatel Space and Astrium are being filled with new commissions.

And then there is the space that locates, that watches over the earth and its inhabitants. Two specialities which suit Toulouse down to the ground. The famous Argos beacons first of all, which can follow anything that moves on our planet: migrating birds, salmon, brown bears from the Pyrenees, ships from the merchant navy, icebergs, you name it! Their precious data is relayed by satellite and compiled, once again, by CLS Argos, providing scientists with incomparable analytical

The Cité de l'Espace in Toulouse, a place of educational discovery unique in France which boasts many fascinating exhibitions *(centre)*.

One of the telescopes of the Pic du Midi Observatory in Bigorre oriented towards the immensity of the universe *(above)*.

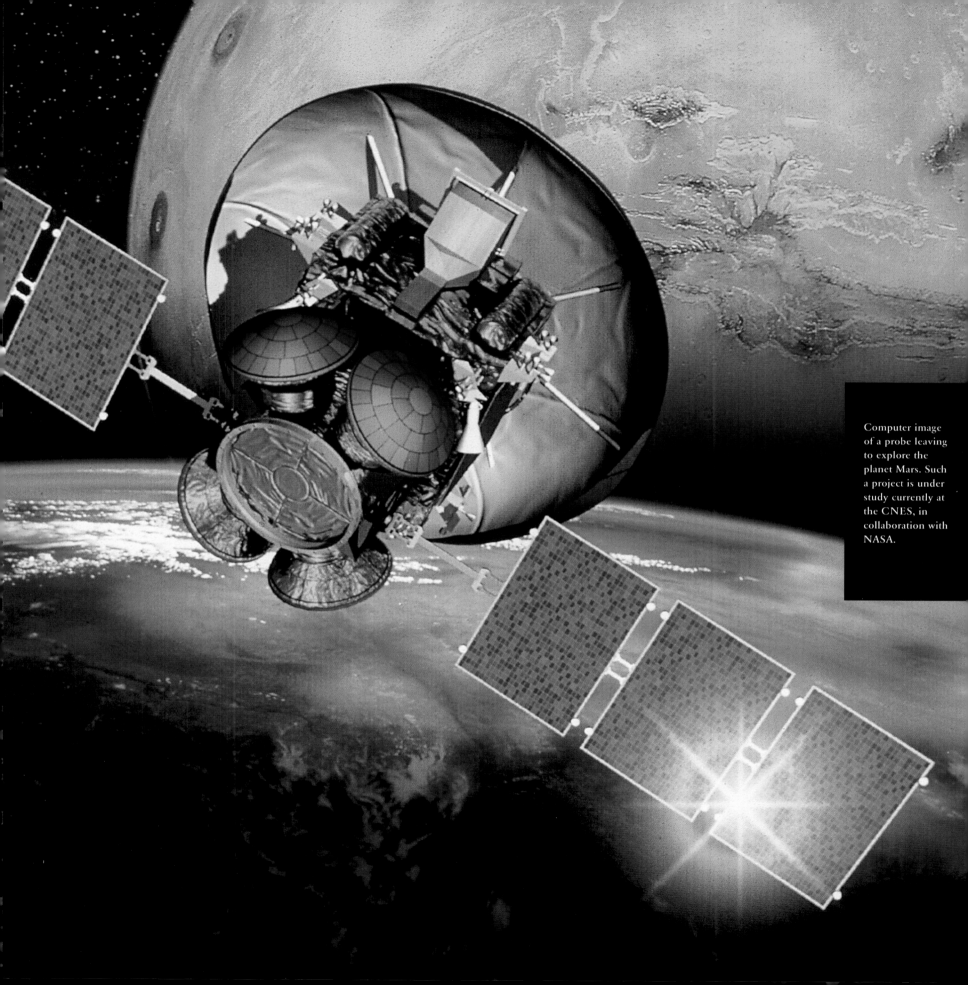

Computer image of a probe leaving to explore the planet Mars. Such a project is under study currently at the CNES, in collaboration with NASA.

tools. In the case of distress signals from isolated voyagers, it is the instruments on board the Copsas-Sarsat system which go into action. These vital messages are received in space then relayed to the nerve centre of CST, the central command system. This is where the rescue help will be sent from, once the caller's position has been precisely pinpointed. More than twelve thousand sailors, mountaineers and miscellaneous adventurers have been assisted in this way since 1982.

Space can lead us to a better understanding of the universe with the hope of gaining more knowledge of the history of our world, of collecting clues on our origins. This is the work of astrophysicists, direct descendants of the astronomers from the observatories at the Pic du

The biggest European launcher, *Ariane V*, blasting off from the Kourou base in Guyana *(far left)*.

Perfected at the CNES in Toulouse, this Mars exploration vehicle will make it possible to collect samples of the planet that will subsequently be sent back to earth for analysis *(left)*.

Midi in Bigorre and at Jolimont. At the CESR (Centre for studies into space radiation), specialists are exploring one of the great astronomical enigmas of our time: "gamma-ray bursts", these violent but mysterious explosions at the very boundaries of our universe. At the Midi-Pyrénées observatory, a galaxy of experts with as many different approaches – geophysics, planetology, cosmology... – are all working towards a deeper understanding of our planet.

Space as a habitat, that goes without saying. Starting with Jean-Loup Chrétien in 1982, the CNES has selected several "spationauts" to experience life in zero gravity on board the Russian *Mir*, the American space shuttle, or the new international space station. For each mission, a whole team of "guardian angels" is formed around the Toulouse CST site to watch over the spationauts before, during and after the flight: co-

Spationauts wear a different badge for each new space mission: this one corresponds to the Antarès mission on board the *Mir* space station.

If greater Toulouse has become the European space capital, you can be sure that its inhabitants are also more tuned into the stars than elsewhere…

ordination of the physical preparation in Moscow or Houston, monitoring of the different stages of the mission, psychological, medical and gastronomic supervision – the catering school in Souillac takes an active part in French "gastronautics"! The MEDES, an institute of spatial medicine and physiology based in Toulouse, has gained universal recognition for its analysis of the effects of weightlessness on the human body.

Lastly, space as a place of exploration, which opens the way to the craziest dreams, in which we discuss landing on and exploring Mars. At the Toulouse branch of the CNES the great adventure is being prepared jointly with NASA. Engineers are actively contributing to so-called "automatic" missions, where little robots explore the red planet in order to study its seasons and atmosphere and even bring back samples of its soil to earth. All this with a view to a human mission in fifteen, twenty, maybe thirty years…

Will the first human on Mars be from Toulouse? Why not? If greater Toulouse has become the European space capital, you can be sure that its inhabitants are also more tuned into the stars than elsewhere… The only question is: do they know it? It seems obvious that this ambience, omnipresent, must have made an indelible imprint on younger minds. How can one avoid dreaming of the exploits of astronauts such as Jean-François Clervoy, a former pupil of Supaéro, the great aeronautics and space college situated at the heart of the scientific complex at Rangueil? How can a child remain unmoved by a parent or friend enthusing about the preparation of elements for a forthcoming probe to Saturn?

The Cité de l'Espace is of course the outward manifestation of this spatial identity. This centre for the diffusion of space culture was inaugurated in 1997 and welcomes 300,000 visitors a year. It endeavours to answer the two fundamental questions – What is space for? and How does it work? – by means of a unique set of interactive exhibitions, films and planetarium programmes. For culture is also scientific, and we have an obligation in the contemporary world to extend it; the evolution of science and technologies brings with it a new comfort and speed, but also certain rights. The right to know, among other things, "how it works"… ■

A view of Montauban taken by Spot. This earth observation satellite, born in Toulouse, makes it possible to chart our planet *(below)*.

The Argos beacon, created by the Toulouse company Collecte et localisation par satellite, has a double function of alerting and locating: this seal will be followed in its migration *(bottom)*.

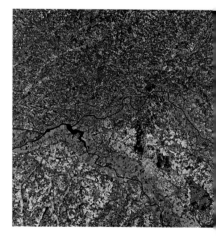

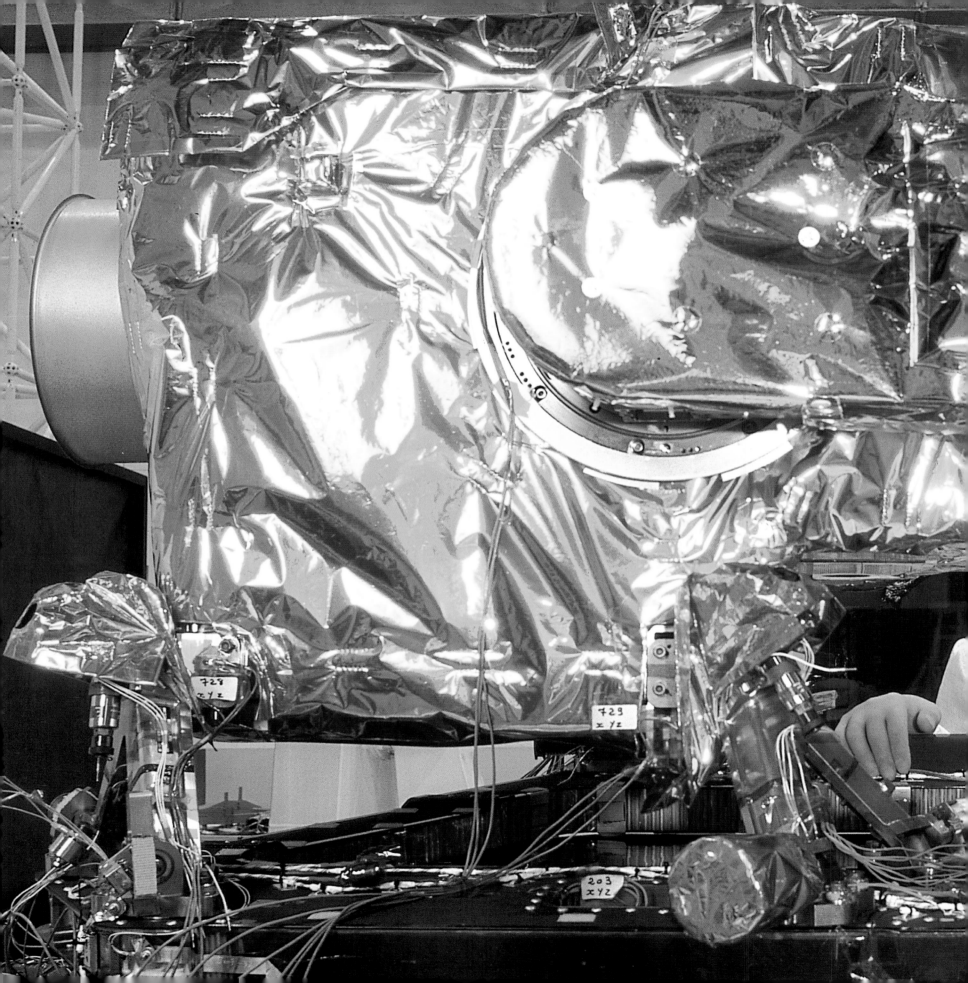

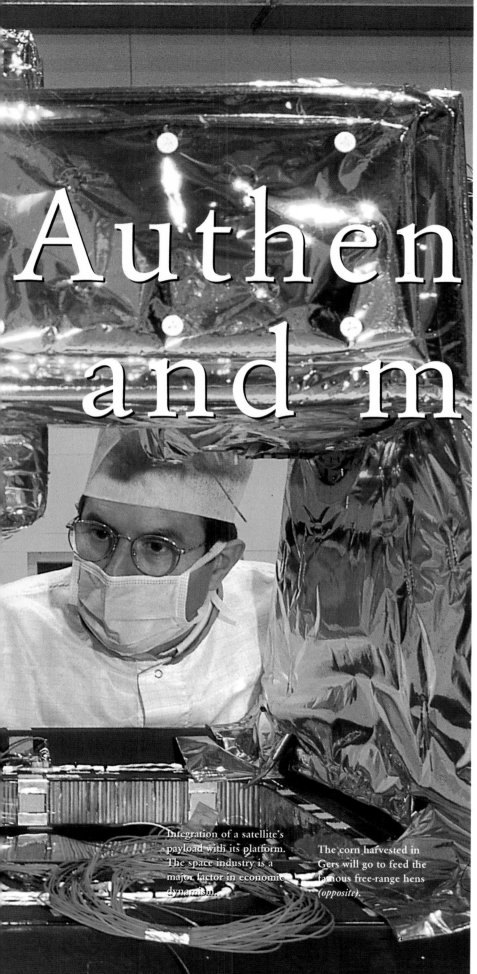

Fabrice Gouze
*Consultant and specialist
in territorial development*

Authentic and modern

FROM THE *CAUSSES* OF QUERCY AND ROUERGUE to the summits of the Pyrenees, from the hills of Gascony to the plains of Lauragais, Midi-Pyrénées has a multitude of faces. They are the result of man's age-old shaping of the land. What emerges is the vitality of agriculture, the dynamism of industry and the enrichment of the environment. Seeing an area through its landscape is a means of enhancing one's appreciation of its character and its economy. We shall use landscape as our mirror.

Integration of a satellite's payload with its platform. The space industry is a major factor in economic dynamism.

The corn harvested in Gers will go to feed the famous free-range hens *(opposite)*.

Alternating fields of corn and Tarbes haricots create an effect of green geometry in the heart of Bigorre *(above)*.

Among the natural resources of Midi-Pyrénées are the rich supply of timber in the Pyrenees *(left)*, and slate, which is a speciality of Labassère, in the Hautes-Pyrénées *(above)*.

Midi-Pyrénées is a land of contrasts: a combination of relief and varying types of exploitation of the soil have produced a great variety of landscapes – high mountains, plains, valleys and *causses* – and therefore an equally great variety of cultivated areas. This rural area covers 90% of the territory in the region and contains 40% of the population.

Agriculture is of prime importance. The proportion of agricultural workers in the active population (about 8%) and the contribution of agriculture to regional GDP represent a total percentage almost double that of the national average. This emphasis on agriculture is even more marked in certain *départements* of the region. In Gers, one in five jobs is in agriculture. In Aveyron, Lot and Tarn-et-Garonne the proportion is about 13%. Overall, agricultural land is devoted fairly evenly to stock rearing (30% grass, 20% fodder plants) and to permanent crops (vineyards, orchards) or annual crops (mainly cereals and oleaginous plants).

These activities take place in a multiplicity of small agricultural entities and in an environment dominated by difficult natural conditions: 95% of the area is classed as mountainous or disadvantaged (lack of water supplies, poverty of the soil). These

Agriculture in the region enters the 21st century determined to be even more attentive to the wishes and expectations of consumers.

conditions have produced an extensive, diversified agriculture which has come to concentrate on quality. Today, more than fifty products bear a quality label which protects and preserves traditional savoir-faire: Appellation d'origine contrôlée, Label Rouge, organic produce, etc. Regional agriculture can therefore enter the 21st century better able to satisfy the demands and expectancies of the public, particularly with regard to food safety and traceability. Such labelling meets with the approval of gastronomes throughout the world, and these products are ambassadors for local culture and tradition. Meat (farm-bred calves, raised with the mother, Aubrac farm-bred oxen, Barèges-Gavarnie sheep), cheese (Causses bleu, Laguiole, Roquefort, Rocamadour, Perail) and wines (Côtes-de-Saint-Mont, Côtes du Frontonnais, Madiran,

Tarn-et-Garonne apples, a high resolution image of Toulouse taken by *Spot V*, a TER regional express train entering a station and Roquefort cheese: technology and agriculture are very closely linked.

Cahors, Gaillac) are some of the products benefiting from the labels. Not to mention the Tarbes haricot, Lautrec pink garlic, Reine-Claude plums and many other flavoursome foodstuffs.

Pastoralism and agriculture are also activities which contribute to the upkeep of the countryside, including its fallow land, and maintain its organisation and harmony. They are therefore of prime importance in conserving and developing regional tourist potential. For there is no doubt that Midi-Pyrénées has a cultural heritage to preserve, and to discover. A new type of traveller has emerged: fleeing the over-populated seaside, he wishes to understand the world which surrounds him, to rediscover his roots and his identity. And the answers to his quest for truth and values are here. He needs only examine the traces left in this area by centuries of civilisation, savour the many faces of the countryside, discover the rich heritage of local culture and architecture, marvel at the diversity of natural milieux, live with the people and join in their characteristic sports. Structured, co-ordinated and developed as they have been, these elements are there to be seen.

Toulouse-Blagnac airport deals with intensive air traffic, both national and international *(above)*.

Infrastructure development has to keep pace with the booming economy. The construction of the A20 at Souillac *(below)*.

There are the great regional sites: Conques, jewel of Roman art; Moissac and its cloister on the road to Santiago de Compostela; Montségur, "the lofty citadel"; Rocamadour, with its series of religious edifices restored by Viollet-le-Duc; Saint-Bertrand-de-Comminges, Flaran, Cordes-Sur-Ciel, the Templar cities of Larzac, Saint-Cirq-Lapopie, the Canal du Midi… and Toulouse with all the richness of its heritage. Then there is the environment: mountains, valleys and *causses* have developed hiking and other outdoor activities (canoeing, mountain biking, rock climbing, paragliding), which make the Midi-Pyrénées a centre valued equally by those seeking strong sensations and those who wish to enjoy their leisure time. More recently a new form of tourism concentrating on scientific technology and discovery has emerged, with visits to places like the cellars at Roquefort, Aerospatiale, the industrial glassworks at Albi and the Pic du Midi observatory.

Tourism has become a major economic activity, making a vital contribution in terms of revenue, employment (more than 20,000 permanent jobs) and territorial development, as well as affirming and propagating the cultural identity of the Midi-Pyrénées region.

For a long time, Midi-Pyrénées only played a limited role in national economic development. If you look at today's countryside, you don't see much effect of the 19th century industrial revolution. What there is is concentrated around specific local resources and savoir-faire. For example the coal mining regions of Carmaux and Decazeville; traditional centres of the textile industry like Castres, Mazamet and Lavelanet; the leather industry in Graulhet and Millau; the cheeses of Roquefort. In the Pyrenees the presence of various metals – lead, copper, zinc, aluminium, manganese – has generated numerous mining developments which survive thanks in great part to the railway and hydroelectric power.

The great change occurred in the sixties with the transfer to Toulouse of the Centre for Space Research at Brétigny, followed by the aviation colleges ENSAE, ENSICA and ENAC. Subsequently, a long list of prestigious firms such as Motorola, Siemens, Alcatel Space and Matra Marconi Space decided to set up in Midi-Pyrénées bringing the industrial and economic resources it had lacked. Today aeronautics and space research are major contributors to the industrial scene through the employment they provide (19,000 salaried workers, 12% of the national work force in this sector) and the sub-contracting they engender – particularly in metallurgy, in the transformation of metals, and in the electrical and electronic industries. They are also important because of the image and reputation they project throughout the world. This orientation has now been strengthened with the choice of Toulouse as the centre for the production of the future large aircraft, the A380. But regional industry is not limited to these two activities; others are important internationally, although not as publicised by the media. Midi-Pyrénées is one of the leading regions in electronics, for instance,

This stratospheric hydrogen balloon belonging to the CNES contributes to the study of the ozone layer *(right)*.

A vehicle equipped with a sophisticated computer guidance system, perfected by Siemens VDO Automotive *(below)*.

In the countryside, the 19th century industrial revolution was concentrated in a few areas, around specific local resources or aptitudes.

in the production of components (Motorola, Siemens, VDO Automotive, Thales, Thomson, CSF, Microturbo, Rockwell Collins); in information technology too, with computer engineering and software creation (Cap Gemini, Transiciel, Storagetek and the Altran Group); in health (Pierre Fabre and Sanofi), chemistry (SNPE, Elf, Atochem, Weishardt) and farm produce (Andros, 3A, Nutrition et Santé and Roquefort Cellars).

In biotechnology, there has been a recent explosion of start-ups, particularly in the bio-medical field, but also in agronomy, in the environment and even in beauty care. The result? In thirty years Toulouse has experienced one of the most rapid growths of any great French city, both demographically and in terms of employment. It is

the fourth city of France and the fifth national urban zone[1], with 920,000 inhabitants, ahead of Bordeaux.

Traditionally industries developed in isolation, but these modern, high-tech "new industries" flourish on proximity – sign of a new economic culture which rejects too clear a separation between the economic and the social spheres. This new practice has spread throughout the region. It applies both to local systems of production by which firms working in the same field and drawing from one employment pool are structured, and to the subcontracting by the major groups of their technological side to small and medium-sized firms which rely on the potential of IUTs (technical colleges) as well as local technical and professional lycées. Within this new dynamic, the universities, *grandes écoles* specialising in engineering, and research

In thirty years Toulouse has experienced one of the most rapid growths of any French city.

A bottling plant in Lot. Viticulture is an important attraction in Midi-Pyrénées.

This huge (18 m long) Laguiole knife designed by Philippe Starck is a symbol of the success of this Aveyron firm.

The Ratier firm at Figeac manufactures propellers in the heart of "Mechanical Valley".

Jeans are not the sole prerogative of America, as is proved by the Liberto firm, which manufactures jeans in Albi.

1. Urban zone: a group of communities consisting of an urban centre and surrounding communities in which 40% of the active resident population in employment work in the urban centre.

laboratories play a vital role. Midi-Pyrénées comes second, after Île-de-France, for numbers of students (110,000) and fourth for the number of university researchers (5,000) and for enterprise in scientific research. All this is due to aid from the state and from the Conseil Régional to the laboratories of the great national organisations (CNRS, INRA, INSERM, CNES, and CERT-ONERA). These large organisations themselves have recently been setting up centres of research and development. Putting this potential for excellence at the disposal of regional companies represents a real challenge for the area's leaders. They must create centres of exchange, areas of solidarity where human communities take advantage of their links to exploit the material and non-material assets at their disposal. To take an example: by creating an "incubator", the object of which is to encourage the creation of innovative firms based on scientific or technological

The Clement-Ader factory, where Airbus's widebody aircraft are produced, is open to the public *(opposite)*.

The reputation of Toulouse's universities attracts thousands of youngsters. Here we see a lecture hall in the Faculty of Social Sciences *(below)*.

research, the Conseil Régional of Midi-Pyrénées has given the participants the means to realise their ambition.

To all who visit I would say: wherever you go, you will be able to evaluate the progress made in our region by studying the landscape. There is no lack of assets or potential in Midi-Pyrénées. Its history has enabled it to avoid painful industrial upheavals. Its geography has obliged it to keep to an extensive agricultural system, concentrating on quality goods.

Grey matter is its number one resource, so its future is in its own hands. Of course there are challenges to be faced, such as those presented by territorial readjustment, but this southern region is dynamic and open to new possibilities. Moreover, people and firms know what they are doing. Ten thousand new inhabitants are settling here every year.

The greatest challenge is probably to welcome these newcomers while preserving the quality of life which makes the region famous. It is likely that habitat and life style will in future be topics of intense debate. What new utopia is going to replace that of the sixties, with its huge sky-rises? Extensive suburbanisation? In this the landscape will again be our mirror – and a merciless one! ■

A PERMANENT SPECTACLE

Midi-Pyrénées, the most extensive region in France, stretches over the south-western heartlands with Toulouse as its capital city. Taking every opportunity for revelry and famed for its welcome and hospitality, it enjoys an enviable climate which prompts one to seek shade in the middle of summer and fills café terraces well into the autumn. Quoted as the region where the quality of life is best and where people live longest, Midi-Pyrénées is also famous for the permanent spectacle offered by its landscapes: summits reaching 3,000 metres; the valleys of Gers with their peculiarly Italian elegance;

Riches of the past: the church of Montsaunès in Haute-Garonne, with its remarkable sculptures of human heads *(left)* and the grotto of Mas-d'Azil, in Ariège *(bottom left)*.

Walking, skiing…The Pyrenees offer a wide range of leisure activities *(centre)*.

the hint of romance in the Montagne Noire; the stone bestiary at Sidobre; natural parks filled with rare treasures; cool rivers beneath burning cliffs; the high, savage plateau of Aubrac... A favourite meeting place of walkers and nature lovers, the region offers 17,000 kilometres of paths, with always something new to discover. Never lacking imagination when it comes to satisfying people's need for leisure activities or their craving for knowledge, Midi-Pyrénées is a reservoir of ideas: a weekend strolling through the streets of Toulouse with the fire of its red brickwork on all sides and dazzling Airbuses overhead; a carefree jaunt in Gers, home of Armagnac, warm hearts and jazz; a few days in the Pyrenees to gaze in awe at the Pic du Midi observatory or the Cirque de Gavarnie; a stroll through Ariège to take in the history of the Cathars or of Roman art; a diversion to Aveyron to view some of the most beautiful villages in France; the paths of Santiago de Compostela in springtime... Or else you can enjoy the prospect of a cruise on the Canal du Midi (regarded by UNESCO as part of a worldwide heritage) or a breathtaking descent of

The beauty of the Lot landscape attracts numerous artists. The sculptor Zadkine settled in Arques, where his works are displayed in a gallery *(above)*.

A gathering place for believers and the sick, Lourdes has become an international centre of pilgrimage *(far left)*.

Some prefer to descend the pistes of Piau Engaly. The Pyrenees are an inestimable economic resource for the region *(opposite)*.

For tourists, the gorges of the Dourbie in Aveyron are a starting place for sensational canoe descents *(below)*.

A haven for walkers and nature lovers, the region offers 17,000 kilometres of paths, with always something new to discover.

the Lot or the Baïse. To those who perpetually seek to enlarge their horizons, Midi-Pyrénées offers numerous theme circuits: the route of the great sites (Rocamadour, Conques, Saint-Bertrand-de-Comminges); the gastronomic route, which allows you to talk to producers while tasting the minor miracles of the locality (foie gras, cassoulet, farm-bred lamb, Roquefort, Chasselas, wines from Cahors or Gaillac). Or the route of the bastides, steeped in history, with its half timbered houses and colourful markets baking in the southern sun. Small wonder, then, that in 2000 the region attracted more than 80,000 visitors.

The variety of experiences offered by tour operators such as Fram, which has its headquarters in Toulouse, encourages the spread of tourism within the region and well beyond its boundaries. Favourite centres are the "départements" of Haute-Garonne and Hautes-Pyrénées, followed by Aveyron and Lot. The main attraction in Hautes-Pyrénées is the possibility of a visit to Lourdes; the famous city and its miraculous grotto continue to attract large numbers of religious tourists.

An estimated 5.5 million pilgrims make the journey to Lourdes per year. Hautes-Pyrénées is also a favourite with skiers (24 stations throughout the valleys and summits of the chain) and with those wishing to take the waters. Health spas are a regional speciality: with more than 75,000 people coming to take the waters every year, Midi-Pyrénées ranks fourth in the range of French thermal regions. Dealing with a modern clientele which is both varied and demanding,

Midi-Pyrénées has become the favoured destination of those who see their holidays as an opportunity to let go, recharge their batteries, enjoy themselves, learn, laugh, and marvel at the delight afforded by daily contact with like-minded people.

Jean-Claude Souléry
Journalist

Cousins as close as brothers

He ALWAYS USED TO SIT exactly in the same place, at the end of the bench. Weariness seemed to fill his gaze, but his words growled like old storms. He wore a dark cap, though not as dark as his eyes. Every evening, his mumbling seemed to go over some old tale, over and over again. Bit by bit, others joined him, who looked like him; some sat on green chairs from the public garden, others unfolded camp-chairs, and they all sat facing the bench, in a garrulous circle, unfolding newspapers and rattling on at great speed. They spoke a language that had a kinship with ours, but which I did not yet understand, with a rumbling, at times extravagant, accent that slowed and lingered at the end of sentences; I marvelled that anyone could speak so fast, but like everyone else, I knew that,

French and Italian farm labourers, threshing at Mousse, in Gers, in the early 1940s.

The pieds-noirs, who arrived in the mid 1960s, set out to modernise agriculture in Midi-Pyrénées *(right)*.

Spanish freedom-
fighters wearing
German helmets,
parading in front of
Toulouse war-memorial
on 3rd September 1944
(above).

During the Franco
dictatorship, republican
refugees published their
papers in France
(centre).

Learning flamenco at
Maite's dance academy,
a flourishing tradition
(bottom).

everyday, the Spaniards gathered in the park, where, inevitably, they dis-agreed hotly over football and deplored the treacherousness of history. One of them, who was sixty, lived longer than the others, long enough to explain to me that, thirty years earlier, fate had catapulted him from the Aragon front onto Place Wilson, which the inhabitants of Toulouse preferred to call "square Wilson".

That was at the end of the 1950s. In those days, there was still a bullring in Toulouse; dustbins stank. In little bars of the Saint-Georges district and Jean-Jaurès avenue, one drank wine standing at the counter. On Place Belfort, one came across more Spaniards, anarchists, talented tailors and refugees who still believed that they would not be staying on. Anyone who bothered to lend an ear realised that Spanish was the main language spoken on Place Wilson, where nowadays one is likelier to hear English.

No-one knows exactly how many Spaniards crossed the Pyrenees northwards in 1939, after the debacle that marked the end of the Span-ish Civil War. They flowed north, in packed columns that frightened the inhabitants of the region and the public authorities, who sensed in these crowds a premonition of future inflows of refugees. They were so poor, and so "red", so strongly associated with leftwing politics, that quaranti-ning them off in camps seemed initially to be the only thing to do. Bit by bit, they scattered, in smaller groups, driven by affinity and, mainly, economic need to seek work in local industrial centres, such as Carmaux and Decazeville, where there were jobs and, usually, a "Café Madrid", to Toulouse, which became their capital-in-exile. It all took time. They rolled up their sleeves and worked in the fields, in steel factories and workshops, breaking off to plunge once again into guerrilla warfare and the camaraderie of the maquis, during the anti-Nazi resistance. Still it took time. They had children, who went to school, became fluent in French, the language of exile. Families grew larger; hard work brought success. Finally, the suitcases and bundles of exile put out roots and their owners became fully-fledged citizens of France. In 1981, there were still in France some 49,000 Spaniards who were officially registered as "refugees": the socialist government suppressed that status, which made them strangers in our midsts. No doubt this was essentially a symbolic measure; but it broke the last link with those distant battles. Perhaps it made it possible for memory to go through with its healing process and ensure, not forgetfulness, but remembrance.

Have they forgotten? So many children were born, so many grandchildren too. Love has diluted regrets and resentment, bringing these ageing Spaniards into the company of French daughters- and sons-

Now and again, they return to Murcia or the banks of the Ebro, to the land of yesteryear's cemeteries, but they all know that their life now lies elsewhere. Here.

in-law. Beyond the Pyrenees lies their homeland; now and again, they return to Murcia or the banks of the Ebro, to the land of yesteryear's cemeteries, but they all know that their life now lies elsewhere. Here.

Here, in Midi-Pyrénées, they have been our village electrician, they have enlivened the evening lull, pushing back the night. Many cafés are run by Spaniards, avenues have become as lively and colourful as Spanish ramblas. Scars obtained in the course of corridas have created a kinship: those people who came from the south are our blood-brothers. That is how the south-west of France definitely acquired the reputation of being a Latin province. Well before Spanish refugees flocked there in the mid twentieth century, waves of Italians had moved

"Square" Wilson, at the beginning of the 1950s, where Spaniards used to meet nearly every evening under Goudouli's pensive gaze *(above)*.

Aficion: a love of bullfighting was part of a way of life in Toulouse, thanks to the presence of a Spanish community, already in the early 1930s *(top right)*.

Selling snails during a popular fête organised by Republican refugees, in Toulouse's Jardin des Plantes *(opposite)*.

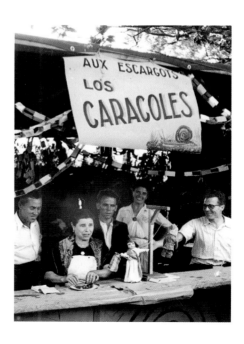

The Bovero family, which settled in Gers in 1930. Their children married into French families. The youngest grand-daughter does not know Italy *(below)*.

Christian Califano, a well-known, Italian-born prop forward of Toulouse's rugby team, Stade toulousain *(bottom)*.

in by the thousands, settling in rural areas: back in Italy, they had heard that the Garonne plains were fertile and generous for those who knew how to work the land. Official notices that read like a general conscription had been posted up outside the town halls of northern Italy, Vazzola, Gradisca, Travagliato, Vespolato, announcing that in the southwest of France, land laid fallow, there was a shortage of manpower, so many men having died in the Great War... Those Italians also knew that the climate was similar to theirs, that people spoke a dialect that resembled their language. And so, from 1920 onwards, Italians began flowing in from Lombardy, alone or in groups, by the trainload, bringing tools and personal belongings, bearing *cassoni,* or chests fastened with rope that they watched constantly since they often contained substantial wealth. The *passaporto* was checked at Vintimille, everyone was vaccinat-

Immigrants insist that they never felt rejected or despised... The smell of *pastasciutta* mingled with the cooking smells of Gascony; those foreigners became neighbours.

ed on crowded platforms, people rushed about in all directions, looking for a lost child, Enzo, or Rita, who turned up in another coach. Everyone knew that the journey's end lay in the countryside. Thus, in 1920, one hundred and forty-four peasant families arrived at Castelsarrasin: wives, children, grandparents, had all come, totalling no less than eight hundred and sixty people. They were pioneers, the first in what became a growing tide of incomers: their enthusiastic discovery of the Garonne valley, the feeling of having reached some kind of paradise, where tomatoes grew as large as cannonballs and the land held out its arms, the prosperity that this seemed to promise, swelled in a rumour that travelled by word of mouth, reaching other regions of Italy and the humblest ears.

That is how poor Italians, owning nothing but their valour, decided to leave their country and the grinding poverty that had been their lot. They were helped to make the leap by the rumours that reached them, and by teams of unscrupulous touts, who travelled up and down Veneto, Piedmont and other provinces, praising the merits of France and encouraging men to travel north to sign up as miners, or south to become farm labourers. Hundreds opted for the south and in 1928, an

Italian *furia* swept through the rural Midi. Were they viewed with distrust? No doubt. Immigrants, though, insist that they never felt rejected or despised. Sometimes, at school, children might call them "Macaronis". Here and there, instances of petty village racism were reported, a few grapes of wrath might turn sour; but, overall, as the smell of *pastasciutta* mingled with the cooking smells of Gascony, those foreigners became neighbours. Locals willingly admitted that the Italians' fields were better weeded and more deeply ploughed than their own, that the overall production of wheat had increased. Other Italians, who had been workmen back in their own country, became masons: to this day, one remembers how they helped to rebuild the Garonne valley, after many of its buildings were washed away in the 1930 flood.

That same year, some 200,000 or so Italians returned to their homeland, lured by fascism and the promises of building projects and social reforms. Others, in contrast, were already considering becoming French, as if they felt that their lakes, landscapes and churches were now too far to return to. The Second World War caused a certain amount of unease. Italians living in France feared reprisals, since Italy was now in the enemy camp. There were none. At the end of the war, many of them obtained French citizenship, anchoring them definitely in their new land. The older members of the community preserved that marvellous accent, women tended to stay at home to bring up their children, who had already lost all idea of their origins and, in the evenings, taught their parents French grammar and vocabulary.

The older men and women never travelled back to the country of their youth. Their children, on the whole, have done well; stories of young masons arriving with nothing but their trowels and rising to become prosperous builders are based on facts. They are no longer Italians, but that does not worry them: nationalism was a relatively recent notion in Italy and did not really mean much. But in their hearts nestles "their" secret corner of Italy, their province, their village, the landscapes they knew, their dialect, home football team and polenta. For the rest, they are inhabitants of Toulouse, Gers, Tarn-et-Garonne.

But what about south of the South? What about those who crossed the Mediterranean instead of the Alps or the Pyrenees? Chased, weary, rejected by history, they arrived, like the others before them, bearing nothing more than a suitcase, rings of weariness darkening their gaze. Thousands of pieds-noirs and harkis arrived from Oran and Algiers; they landed at Toulouse's Blagnac airport and poured onto the platforms of Matabiau station. There were ten thousand or so of them, doomed to start again from scratch. Some were treated with contempt,

The Buzzichelli brothers started from nothing to build up their haulage company into one of the biggest in Haute-Garonne *(above and opposite)*.

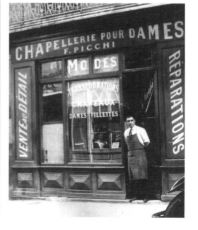

An Italian hat-maker of Toulouse, in the 1940s *(opposite)*.

Rubén Velásquez, a
Toulouse tenor born in
Spain, has worked to
bring the Occitan and
Arab-Andalusian cultures
together *(above)*.

A constant exchange between
north and south, Goethe
discovering Occitan, fast-food
flavoured with cumin, a future
carved out in rail and rock, raï
and rap blending in a new,
cosmopolitan *patois*…

others enjoyed a certain amount of solidarity; all knew that they had no hope of ever returning to where they came from, no choice but to work and start a new life.

They were mostly humble people, petty civil servants, workmen. Some were lucky enough to have relatives on the mainland, who helped them. Those who chose to settle in the towns and countryside of the Midi clung obstinately to the sunshine they had left behind and to their customs. It only took them five years to revolutionise culinary habits in the south-west: restaurants now serve as much couscous with merguez as cassoulet with sausage. These newcomers have blended into the social and cultural landscape, as if they had always been here, except for a touch of bitterness that has mellowed over the years. Older people preserve a lingering trace of an accent which recalls that they were born on the farther shore of the Mediterranean. Soon afterwards, other people from the Maghreb followed, borne by harsh economic necessity on the sirocco that blows north into the vent d'autan of Midi-Pyrénées. To assert that they have found happiness and satisfaction might be wishful thinking, but the tradition of tolerance that has marked the history of our region has so far ensured that social peace is preserved and xenophobic crusades are avoided. It is to be hoped that this lasts.

The Midi has thus opened up to the south, to cultures that are not really that different from ours; and if, in the sixties, they did seem alien, they have since taken root in the Occitan soil and are now part of the landscape. Spanish, Italian, Algerian, Oranese, Kabyle, Occitan and French tongues and tempers make for animated talk, smiles, songs, wines, dances, rugby, bullfighting, love and other pleasures, in empathy with the wind, street-life, hot summer days, russet autumn sunlight, pink brick walls and a melting-pot of accents. In this new kind of tango, danced on a text by Goudouli, a tune by Zebda, and sung by Carlos Gardel, Nougaro and Vicente Pradal, those cultures might easily have become homogeneous, a cousinly, Latinate, medley – except that, in the past two decades, our region has also welcomed newcomers from the misty lands of the north that look southwards, in what seems to be a growing trend.

Centuries ago, barons from the north left hateful memories in Cathar Languedoc, from Albi to Montségur; but the wounds have long since healed. Today's barons are engineers working in aircraft, high-tech and other specialised industries; they come from Britain, Germany and the French regions north of the Loire, bringing science and technology in their luggage. Grey matter is to them what pastel used to be to merchants. Every year, some ten thousand scholars flock south: chemists, computer engineers, specialists in every field, bearing in their pockets names and acronyms that sing a new, technological patois: CNRS, CNES, Airbus, etc. But the southern way of life is catching: they send their children to play rugby, they go climbing in the Pyrenees, they expect a swimming-pool when they buy a house. They are told that they bring to the Midi method, perseverance, efficiency, obstinacy and constancy. In exchange, they discover sunny tempers and talents, the boldness of troubadours and bullfighters, that spark of genius that blossoms in the sun.

Our region blends Latin dreams and northern mores, it has enabled cultures to meet and come together in a constant exchange between north and south, Goethe discovering Occitan, fast-food flavoured with cumin, a future carved out in rail and rock, raï and rap blending in a new, cosmopolitan patois. Those are just a few of the privileges of a land that is inhabited by cousins who are as close as brothers. ■

Reminiscences of Oriental sensuality, with this belly-dancer from the multi-ethnic district of Arnaud-Bernard, Toulouse *(left)*.

Sports knocks down frontiers. Emile Ntamack playing with Stade Toulousain *(top)*, while Irish fans support their team in a Toulouse pub *(below)*.

Paths

# of flavours

Raimon Faure
Journalist

In the land of the gourmet

SMALL MISSHAPEN BOUQUETS with bottle green "flowers", their russet stems, frail and limp, roughly held together by an ageless elastic band: here, on a rickety stall in Rabastens market, with the last of the winter mists reluctant to lift, they do not even catch the eyes of city dwellers out on a jaunt. For the locals, on the other hand, these *respounjous* are harbingers of spring.

Gathered from damp hedgerows and ditches, these odd creepers, easily mistaken for wild asparagus, were baptised *tamus communis* or *tamier* by botanists and "battered wives' herbs" by jealous husbands who, incapable of mending their

Goose foie gras can be identified by its attractive pinky-white complexion. Half-cooked, served on a piece of toast with pepper and salt, it is a real delicacy *(above)*.

Potted goose conserve. When removing a piece, take care to cover the remaining morsels with the soft fat in the jar *(opposite)*.

Respounjous, a rare sight on market stalls; its harvesting on Sundays in early spring is a family ritual.

ways, were at least familiar with their property of preventing bruising. Although mentioned by Pliny in his Natural History, their unconditional supporters can now be found only around Albi, Rouergue and Quercy. Despite their extreme bitterness, their most fervent devotees eat them raw in salads but they are more often blanched with a *croustet* of bread before marrying them with eggs in an omelette or the firm tasty white meat of a true farm hen – not to be confused with a supermarket free-range chicken…

For an aperitif or an impromptu snack, pork or duck *charcuterie* is always appropriate *(above)*.

Lautrec pink garlic, whose renown rivals that of the white garlic of Lomagne, is often married with olive oil, adding a touch of the south to regional dishes *(opposite)*.

Gathered from damp hedgerows and ditches, *respounjous* are harbingers of spring.

My reason for evoking these humble *respounjous*, whose strong, pungent taste would hurt the irksome sensibilities of many a modern palate, is that they seem to me to symbolise the original nature of Midi-Pyrénées cuisine. Firstly because of their prehistoric aspect – "paleolithic" was how the great writer of Pieusse, Joseph Delteil of Aude, described them –: a miserable bunch of *respounjous* handed over in exchange for a thousand old francs on a market in Tarn takes us back to our hunting-gathering ancestors. And secondly because they symbolise the overtly rustic character of regional culinary habits (which in no way excludes refinement!), in no hurry to adopt Parisian-style "gastronomy".

For, apart from the exploits of chefs such as Michel Bras, who anyway drew the inspiration for their art from this area, Quercy, Languedoc and Gascony do not seem particularly gifted at the kind of "official" cuisine that seems to rely so heavily on etiquette and appearance. The rel-

Game birds have their aficionados. In the south-west, the mallard is hunted *(opposite)*, along with quails, thrushes, partridges and even, word has it, ortolans!

A calf *élevé sous la mère* means that it was raised exclusively on mother's milk *(below)*.

atively mediocre score attributed to Midi-Pyrénées with respect to its gastronomic character in the Michelin, a sort of little red book on classicism of the table, underlines this state of affairs. The region as a whole undoubtedly suffered from the relative lack of dynamism which characterised its capital, Toulouse, until the middle of the last century; "a big village" the university professor Philippe Wolf was to write… For establishments to exist, flourish and build up a reputation, the exchanges and the customers offered by a large city are crucial.

But history has many cards up its sleeve and with the passing of time, this archaic quality has opened up a door of opportunity. The culture of simplicity at the table calls for ingredients of exceptional quality: the less sophisticated the treatment, the less one can disguise the basic flavour. More than anywhere else, restaurants have maintained supply

sources close to the countryside, close to nature. Well after the *brilliant* invention of battery hens, for example, one can still find authentic poultry in markets here, with sturdy muscles and a good, strong flavour. Other examples of authentic produce include the succulent *milk calves* and magnificent beef cows with marbled meat which have contributed to the renown of the Montréjeau, Saint-Girons and Laissac meat markets... And the fat of the black Gascon pork with its delicate aroma of fresh hazelnuts, native cousin to the prestigious Andalusian *patas negras* ... And, thanks to the very eminent patronage of the Lacaune hills, the Tarn or Aveyron lambs which, rumour has it, end their career somewhere near Sisteron...

Left to right:
Lambs from Quercy, the Pyrenees or Lacaune constitute the traditional Easter dinner.

Free-range grey hens from Gers.

The black pig of Gascony feeds mainly on grasses and acorns.

While basic ingredients constitute a rich communal picking pot, ways of preparing them are, on the contrary, extremely varied.

Such is the importance placed on authentic produce in Midi-Pyrénées that in 1992, an organisation, Irqualim, was founded, with the support of the public authorities, charged with cataloguing, protecting and promoting original regional farm produce and indicating its quality in one of three labels: AOC, Label rouge or IGP. To date, fifty products benefit from this system, from the Lautrec pink garlic to the Tarbes haricot, from the *chasselas* grape of Moissac to the Rocamadour *cabécou*, from the Quercy melon to Roquefort.

And yet, while these basic elements are common to all, each corner of Midi-Pyrénées has very different ways of preparing them and totally opposing traditions; this very lack of consistency, which generates a colourful mosaic of flavours, can be seen as one of the region's specificities. We could be tempted to write, in true journalese, of a "land of contrasts", but a "land of confluence" would be closer to the truth. One example above all others symbolises the intermingling of opposing influences: fat. "Fat is flavour" we are taught in catering schools, of which Midi-Pyrénées boasts some nationally renowned establishments. And fat comes in all forms and flavours here, each variety adding its signature to the dishes it inspires.

Let us start with goose or duck fat: André Daguin, a native of Auch, who invented among other things *magret* (duck or goose cutlets), turned this family secret and unquestioned source of good health into a icon of Gascony, associating it with garlic for "*doping* soups", marrying

Shelled by patient hands then peeled, these beans, to be eaten raw dipped in salt, are a delicacy *(above)*.

This generous lady is showing off her honeyed melons from the nearby slopes *(opposite)*.

Black or white, the first chasselas grapes are bursting with juice *(right)*.

Thanks to the classification attributed to fifty products in Midi-Pyrenees (AOC, Label rouge and IGP), the paths of the gourmet are henceforth well-traced. Goose and duck foie gras aside, the uncontested heroes of regional gastronomy are the free range poultry of Gers, raised on grain, and the beef cows of Gascony, which graze on the foothills of the Pyrenees and in Ariège. The salted meats of Lacaune, emblematic of the black mountains, can hold their own against Andalusian jabugo, and local lamb, raised freely on the causses of Larzac and the Pyrenees, easily matches up to that of Pauillac or Sisteron. Veal from Aveyron and Ségala (a region straddling Aveyron, Tarn and Lot) is raised "under the mother", which lends its flesh an unequalled tenderness and flavour. Try the speciality dishes cassoulet, garbure, aligot, estofinade, and the cheeses Roquefort, Bleu des causses, Tomme from the Pyrenees and Laguiole – which have pride of place on the very best cheese platters. For dessert, treat yourself to a croustade from Bagnères-de-Bigorre or a Gascon pastis and if you are tempted by the fruit basket, a Lectoure or Quercy melon or a bunch of chasselas grapes from Moissac. Finish up with some mouth-watering boiled sweets from Cauterets, every child's favourite treat.

it with meats, eggs or fish. Here is a tip to convince you of its powers: take some fat from around the foie gras, mince a garlic clove from Beaumont de Lomagne and a dozen chervil stems, mix together and add to fresh pasta, cooked *al dente* (the influence of the thousands of Italians who flocked to Gascony in the 1930s). Certain other animal fats also find favour with cordon bleu chefs in Midi-Pyrénées, although to a much lesser extent: lard – quite naturally in a region which produces so

The truffle,
Quercy's black
diamond.
A simple but
delicious
traditional recipe
sets it with egg in
a kind of omelette
called a *brouillade*.

From izard haunches to red partridge casserole, game has pride of place in festive meals.

many magnificent pigs – and butter, in general unpasteurised, especially if it comes from the high Pyrenean pastures or the dry grasses of the *causses*, wreathed in rare perfumes.

At the other end of the range, walnut oil is a great speciality of the Quercy and Rouergue regions; its sensitivity to sources of light and heat is matched only by its elegant bouquet. One must treat it with respect, never cook it but use it as a basis, along with fresh walnuts, pink garlic

and parsley, for an *aillade*, a wonderful *aïoli* with the scents of the Massif Central which so perfectly accompanies farm veal cutlets or even some well desalted stockfish.

The other great oil used in Midi-Pyrénées cuisine is olive oil; this is not to say that olive groves have suddenly replaced Castelsarrasin apple orchards or Laguépie chestnuts, but quite simply that Toulouse, the historic capital of Languedoc, has attracted Mediterranean popula-tions – Catalans, Narbonnese, not to mention the Italians already referred to and the Spanish in 36 – who have brought with them their southern tastes.

If you wish to discover how this melting-pot works, coat some toasted bread with olive oil and add the heady flavour of fine slices of black truffle from Lot or Ariège; in general, the magic works and the combination a success.

A stockfish for some salt. This exchange, employed in years gone by on Nordic sailing boats, accounts for the presence of *estofinado* in Rouergue *(above)*.

Conserves piled up like treasures in the pantry of a Gers abode *(left)*.

Truffles link into an important section on hunters-gatherers, already brought up with regard to *respounjous*, even if their "cultivation" and harvest demand some human intervention. In this category can be placed cepe and chanterelle mushrooms from the August storms, morels from the thawing of the snow, icy juniper seeds which will go to heat up some tender rabbit, wild lettuces and aromatic herbs, sloes, blackberries and other fruits of the forest. And of course game, a controversial subject, but so rooted in the culinary habits of a region which has always kept at least one foot on the ground. From izard haunches to red partridge casserole, from wild boar stew to deer filets: game birds, game animals and even game fish (small black trout and pikeperch) occupy pride

Red, white or rosé, Midi-Pyrénées wines are a must at table.

of place in all Midi-Pyrénées festive tables. And what about the story of the prefect who turned up in the countryside as noisily as possible as the locals were indulging in their favourite sport, ortolan hunting? The story goes that he wanted to tip them off, unofficially of course, as to the arrival of a newly appointed public prosecutor, a stickler for the rules…

From *respounjous* to ortolans, what a singular path we have come: from a humble creeper to a bird of Virgilian bitterness that was said to have been a favourite delicacy of certain heads of state. Perhaps this is the true story of Midi-Pyrénées' cuisine, this cuisine of confluence which, rather than being impoverished by its mixtures, stands enriched. ∎

In their now dry pods, the Tarbes haricots are *brilliante ma non troppo*, as if they had been waxed *(above)*.

The oval ball, a symbol of a way of life typical of the south-west *(opposite)*.

The Tarbes haricot

Raimon Faure
Journalist

Budding champion

TO KICK OFF WITH, SOME APOLOGIES. To Jean Gachassin, a charismatic stand-off half, fidgeting like a black trout from the young Adour river. To Jean-Michel Aguirre, a placid demi-God, escapee on the free side of the Pyrenean Pantheon. And to Jean Prat, a miraculous third-liner, one of those men whose sacrifices are forever sanctified. I humbly beg these three brave warriors and all those others, celebrated or unknown, of Bagnères, F.C. Lourdais and Stadocest rugby clubs, to forgive me, to forgive all of us. For while it is true that we have been known to go crisscrossing the area around Bigorre at weekends, it is not just to keep ourselves warm with the aid of such invigorating afternoon activity, a recipe which many a mountain-bred rugbyman brought up on *monjetada* is privy to, but to go hunting for the missing ingredient of this very magic potion: the bean. And not just any old bean! The Tarbes haricot, an immaculate and exemplary idol of a traditional system of agriculture where the *culture* is as important as the *agri*.

The runner beans are always hand picked, and the stems are trained up a thread *(top)*.

The pack, supreme expression of rugby's team spirit. Here pictured during a France-Ireland match in the 1970s *(above)*.

Indeed, if this bean were to join the ranks of our rugby heroes, its mighty 0.7 grams would contain a concentrate of almost all of the qualities that have led these players to the success our dreams were made of. Firstly, and perhaps most importantly, it does not give itself airs and graces. It has remained true to itself, this little Latino immigrant which disembarked at the end of the 18th century from its native Peru; it hasn't forgotten it was in the business of cheering up very humble plates before going on to play its current starring role in chic Parisian restaurants.

It appreciates team spirit: at table it is more at ease in a family stewpot than in individual plates, and in the fields – on the turf one might almost say… – it is aware that it owes its revival to the joint efforts of all the people from Bigorre making up the Interprofessional Association of the Tarbes haricot. This team has obtained not only the *Label Rouge* but more recently, in order to mount an even better defence for its bean, the IGP (protected geographic indication), a sort of trophy of agricultural authenticity.

One often hears that there is no rugby without peasants, and it must be pointed out that the Tarbes haricot has a very close relationship with the earth. Not the Welsh mud of old Arm's Park, of course, but the lighter, relatively acid (pH of 5 to 6), alluvial earth of the banks of the Adour. Like its cousins the vines (the *tannat*, which gives the great Madiran, or the *cot* from the hills of Cahors), the Tarbes haricot is a child of its land, a land which is contained within Hautes-Pyrénées and a few bordering districts.

Another of its qualities is its good health, so obvious it speaks worlds. This robust specimen, fresh-faced if a mite dented, has not undergone any laboratory manipulation or other dubious modification. Out of the ten varieties of bean classified in the last century, two have been especially encouraged: the *haricot maïs* – which we will come back to later – and above all, the *alaric*, which derived its name from a canalised stream which flows to the east of Tarbes. Smelling reassuringly of Grandad's vegetable patch, both varieties represent excellent dietetic quality: they are rich in carbohydrates (63%) – very important before kick-off! – and in proteins (approximately 23%) but very low in lipids (1%).

They are also brimming over with minerals and trace elements and experiments indicate that they contribute to lowering the cholesterol rate and the risk of cancer of the colon. On the ecological side, they have no need of fertilisers because, like all leguminous plants, beans fix nitrogen from the air in the earth. This explains why they have always been associated with corn which, as a cereal, needs a large amount of nitrogen. The fact of cultivating these two plants alongside each other, according to a method described as early as 1807 by the botanist Augustin Pyramus de Candolle in his *Voyage of Tarbes*, also saves the farmer having to plant hazelnut, chestnut or bamboo rods for this naturally garrulous runner bean.

But let's not beat about the bush, or as they say in Occitan, *de l'oule ou du toupin*: what is it that allows the Tarbes haricot, match after match, to outclass fragile *cocos* (although I do have a soft spot for those of Bonnac, near Pamiers), body-built *soissons* and firm *lingots*? It is on the pitch, sorry the plate, that the difference is perceptible. Before arriving at table, it holds its shape admirably during cooking; all good

> It is on the pitch, sorry the plate,
> that the Tarbes haricot wins us over,
> at that luscious moment when its creamy
> texture, engorged with juice,
> is crushed between tongue and palate.

A beautiful winter's Sunday kicks off with lunch – *cassoulet, monjetadas, estoufets* or any other mouth-watering haricot dish – accompanied by a bottle of some decent Midi-Pyrénées wine, then it's off to the stands of the nearby stadium to support one's own team, although always with the greatest of respect for the other side.

family cooks, women or men (to keep up with the times), will tell you that the Tarbes haricot stays whole, even after twelve hours cooking, as long as it is not whipped around in a maelstrom of stock or stirred incessantly. Paradoxically, this little toughie has the skin of a baby, which can only enhance the succulent moment when the bean's creamy texture, engorged with juice, is crushed between tongue and palate. When discussing a great wine we talk of the "touch of the mouth"; here the expression is amply justified as we appreciate its extreme softness, comparable to the Laguépie chestnut in Tarn-et-Garonne, and the fruity sweetness of its Bigorre neighbours: the impressive Trébons onion and the precious little Asté carrot. To crown it all, unlike most of its competitors it is never floury because low in starch; this is its own special elegance.

We could of course limit the range of its gastronomic qualities to the *cassoulet*, and it is true that simmering it in earthenware pots in a breadmaker's oven along with some choice cuts – Gascon black pig

The final
of the French
championship in
1949 which
featured the
Toulouse "Stade".

Soon after
picking: the
haricots are still
in their husks.

and goose conserve – truly brings out the best of the Tarbes haricot. It has become the uncontested prince of *cassoulet*, for all the qualities already mentioned, and amply deserves to add colour and flavour to all *après-match* festivities. But to restrict it to this one dish seems a mite hasty. Just look at the *monjetadas* which perk up village fetes all round Midi-Pyrénées. Wreathed in childhood aromas, these cassoulets in all but name match the culinary authenticity of the Ariège *estoufets* or *estoufats*, the Tarn *fabonadas* or the Saint-Gaudens *pistaches* where mutton, another Pyrenean speciality, replaces other meats.

Some almost vegetarian versions of these dishes exist, such as corn bean *estoufets* with cod, a dish served traditionally at funerals. For the Tarbes haricot is in its element in many different combinations, not just in cassoulet. With marine flavours for instance. Try the delicate Tarbes haricot soup with cockles and clams invented by chefs

> To restrict the Tarbes haricot to the *cassoulet* is a mite hasty. Look at the *monjetadas* which perk up village fetes all round Midi-Pyrénées.

Gérard Garrigues and Alain Dutournier. Or let yourself be tempted, one wintry morning, by a cream of Tarbes haricot soup with bacon, delicately flavoured with a finger of Souillac walnut liqueur. With top quality produce and the finest basic ingredients (a solid pack and a respect for basics, as they say in rugbyland)… –, imagination sprouts wings.

Just as rugby upsets the logic of superficial souls, the Tarbes haricot could be said to be an aberration, the most delicious of aberrations. The sixties, puffed up with triumphal modernity, could well have signalled for this bean the "coming of the end" that the Bible and the midrashic Jewish tradition have conserved since the time of the great flood. These too archaic Tarbes haricots had to watch their skin – extremely fine as we have already said – faced with technocrats brought up on trashy science-fiction who imagined we would go forward into the third millennium (back to the future!) eating pills. This is how pro-

Earthenware *cassoles*, which gave their name to *cassoulet* (top).

Jean-Louis Bérot, an attacking player, was for a long time in the French "Reds and Blacks" (*opposite*).

183

When shelling the Tarbes haricot, the beans slip between one's fingers like the beads of a rosary *(above)*.

duction which spread over an area of 18,500 hectares in 1880 covered only 5 hectares in 1970, not counting semi-domestic smallholdings. Our bean could almost claim damages from the eulogists of industrial agriculture. The invention of supposedly profitable hybrid corn – and its corresponding chemical herbicides and insecticides – almost dealt it a deadly blow. Luckily Bigorre locals, with much foresight, continued to grow the bean in their vegetable patches until the wind turned and brought it to the attention of haute cuisine. The flip side of this new-found trendiness has been a steep price rise; dry beans can now reach up to 100 francs a kilo in certain chic delicatessen in Paris.

Two points should nevertheless be noted. Firstly, that this natural leguminous plant, grown locally according to traditional techniques and requiring much attention, has always been relatively expensive, as witness the old texts which talk of winegrowers arriving, in Pyrenean Piedmont, to exchange a barrel of their wine against a barrel of haricots; and secondly, that with a kilo of dried Tarbes haricots – plus garlic, pig, goose and mutton – one can feed half of a rugby team. And they say that athletes are all-rounders… ∎

It was in the 1530s that the haricot arrived from what were known as the Indies, to begin its conquest of southern Europe. Olivier de Serres, the inventor of modern agronomy, refers to it as early as 1600 in his "Théâtre d'agriculture" under the name of "faziol", although another century was needed before the haricot supplanted such legumes as beans, chick peas and dolics which were such an important part of the staple diet in rural areas. In 13th century Bigorre, the Tarbes bean became known in association with corn. One should note that the Occitan word "monjet" (haricot), from which the word "monjetada" is derived, actually comes from the dolic, a white Asian bean with a large black umbilicus whose aspect was reminiscent of the habit worn by the Dominicans ("monjas" in Occitan).

Rugby, a ballet of choreography and combat, so propitious to conviviality.

Enhanced by pork, goose, duck or mutton, the Toulouse cassoulet was referred to by Prosper Montagné as the "God of Occitanian cuisine".

Vineyards

Michel Cardoze & Vincent Pousson
Journalists and writers

Cometh the vine cometh the man

Grass has sprung up between the perfectly trimmed rows, proof that the winegrower is acting in harmony with the soil.

Grape-pickers' buckets are heavy with fruit here in Madiran *(opposite)*.

WINES ARE LIKE PEOPLE; SOME STIFFEN and look you up and down, proud certainly, but haughty too. Others come forward, hand outstretched, open and welcoming, with ready sympathy. Popular conception, which is rarely mistaken, places Cahors and Madiran, the two stars of the Pyrenees, in this latter category. They are wines for meeting friends and strangers and for celebrating – joyful table companions for all occasions. At the same time, the touch of elegance furnished by the full body of these robust wines prevents them coming over as too frivolous, tatty or vulgar. As if nature, in order to perfect their culture, had digested and assimilated her own extremes, taking inspiration from the

north wind blowing on the brick-red earth, desiccated by icy cold, of the *causse* of Lalbenque and from the July days when grapes roast on the languishing hilltops of Maumusson-Laguian. The winegrowers of Madiran and Cahors, their perfectionism matched only by their appetite for plan-

The peaks of the Pyrenees provide a backdrop to the Madiran vineyards in the heart of winter *(above)*.

The Château de Viella, where Alain and Christine Bortolussi produce intense black wines *(left)*.

etary conquest, stride out at the head of a motley but recognisable flock rounded up, quivering with pride, from all the wine-growing areas of the Occitan heartlands: Côtes-de-Gascogne, Gaillac, Fronton, Marcillac… Much envied by their Aquitanian neighbours of Buzet, Marmande or Duras they do not, unlike the latter, dream of clinging to the skirts of Bordeaux. For, and this is the crux of the matter, between the Languedoc and Bordeaux wine countries, an archipelago of vineyards has long existed between creases in the earth's crust, Hercynian to the north and Alpine to the south, the soil of which is impregnated with sediment from both sea and river. These wines did not in the past share a clearly defined identity, whether due to a lack of boldness, or to self-interested subservience to famous neighbours, but circumstances gradually combined to produce a change in this situation. There was a quest for typicality, a return to original vines, more rigorous cultivation practices and a refined ageing process. Everywhere wine became more distinguished and Toulouse could serve Madiran and the other wines without feeling

The black *tannat* and its most illustrious champion, winemaker Alain Brumont *(above)*. Late harvesting for the Pacherenc *(bottom right)*. Winemakers from the Saint-Mont wine co-operative, in their prephylloxera vineyards *(bottom left)*.

The profound and paradoxical character of Cahors is expressed in wines with the rough contours of youth which are softened by ageing.

vaguely ashamed. This revolution in vineyards, plots, barrels, vats, processes and palates took place from the mid-1970s on. Today, the results are obvious.

In Cahors there are some tasty little wines, quick to mature, which are promptly married with *charcuterie* from neighbouring Aveyron. But the really profound and paradoxical character of the appellation is expressed in wines with the rough contours of youth, which are softened, rendered more agreeable by ageing. Among the latter, one of the idols of rich, voluble bar mythology is "Vieux Cahors" as it is referred to in awed tones by drinkers of the same ilk, who know it will afford them

licentious enjoyment. A traditional practice in Quercy, which has now almost disappeared, was the *perpétuelle*. This consisted of filling a barrel with a good vintage, which was preserved for several years. The owner would then begin to draw off a little wine for his own consumption and top up the barrel with wine of the current year's vintage. In this way, "old Cahors" initiated the young, the young initiated the younger and so on. With such effect that the *perpétuelle*, originally an innocent wine-making tool, was transformed into a veritable alchemist's crucible in which the peasant of Cahors brewed his share of immortality.

The real quality of Cahors comes from its particular variety of vine, the *auxerrois*, which has been growing for some considerable time

A stock of as yet unripe *auxerrois*. This authentic vine from Lot belongs to the family of *côts*, which also comprises the Madiran *tannat* and the Fronton *négrette*.

in the Lot area. The round, purple grapes it produces are called *malbec* in Bordeaux and *cot* in the Loire, since Francois I attempted to introduce them there. They belong to the large family of *côts*, which includes many cousins, such as the Madiran *tannat* and the Fronton *négrette. Auxerrois* produces black juice and gives the wine its rich tannic quality. When the vintage is of good quality and the whole process of winemaking well conducted, it produces an exceptional mellowness worthy of a fine Pomerol. With ageing, a remarkable bouquet is added, in which black-berry, sloe and violet mingle with the perfume of undergrowth, not to mention the unforgettable flavour of truffle, sublime catalyst of gastro-nomic desires, which adds opulence to refinement.

At Madiran, the jewel of the principality is *tannat*, a combative vine growing between the bare pebbles of the moraines – now hills – of

Erected between the 15th and 16th century on the base of a 12th century stronghold, Château Lagrezette is classed a historic monument. Alain-Dominique Perrin, Cartier's effervescent chairman, is also a Cahors winemaker, producing elegant, smooth wines *(left)*.

the vanished glaciers of the Pyrenees – now plains. This vine nearly dis-appeared in 1958 in favour of the cabernet franc (an imported vine) as a result of the somewhat ill founded advice of the *Institut National des Appellations d'Origine*, which criticised the former's harshness. A few men, a few families, defended the ampelographic heritage and today bottles of 100% *tannat* are fought over and fetch prices – an irony of his-tory this – almost equalling those of the finest Médoc vintages. The other star vine in this corner of Gascony, on the borders of Gers and the Hautes-Pyrénées, is the little *manseng*, which yields intense, sweet whites called pacherenc-du-vic-bilh.

We met Alain Brumont in the early nineties. He struck us as a kind of brilliant descendant of those baroque lords whose volubility and pas-sion, together with their love of pleasure and of the company of others, placed them at the head of the Bullfighting Club of Vic-Fezensac. And

Mathieu Cosse from the Domaine des Laquets reinvents Cahors with all the spirit and daring befitting of the rising generation of winemakers *(above)*.

From left to right:
At Saint-Salvy-de-Coutens, the hills are clad in autumnal splendour.

One of the many dovecotes which pepper the Tarn landscape.

Grapes being picked by hand in Gaillac. When harvested manually, the grape suffers a minimum of interference, thus guaranteeing its quality.

indeed he was to live up to this vision. At the time he was up to his eyes in the work beginning on the Montus cathedral wine cellar. He presided over his table – guests of the day, wife and children, office colleagues and collaborators in the wine trade – played *quillet*, sang the praises of the Tarbes haricot and Sarrancolin marble, discussed his successful initiative in associating clients with the ownership of the underground wine cellar at Bouscassé and outlined plans for a verdant presentation of stories and legends around the history of the vine and wine-making to put the finishing touches to the estate (which I pictured in his hands as an opulent Gallic-Roman villa); the gardens of Bouscassé have since sprung up. All this sincere and energetic public relations effort was possible because Madiran wine bearing the name of Brumont, Montus or Domaine Bouscassé had become an exceptional product, fulfilling the

potential of its regal vine, the *tannat*. The wine had at last been processed and aged in wood, had received praise and medals as it conquered the wine cellars of all continents, and had everywhere been compared favourably with the greatest stars of the French wine constellation, at the head of which Brumont himself had placed the Côte-Rôtie of Monsieur Guigal – whom I met later at a party at Montus, at the same table as Daniel Humair, who had just been improvising on skins stretched between the staves of new barrels.

Two other princes, in this case reigning over the white Gaillac wines, are Robert and Bernard Plageoles, father and son who, in the Domaine des Très Cantous, had the effrontery to invent great new wines while at the same time retaining the heritage of Gaillac. Under their aegis original grapes with sonorous name like *len de l'el, mauzac, ondenc, braucol, duras* or *prunelard* were reborn as dry, creamy or even sweet wines. And now, just as was the case with Cahors and Madiran, bottles of Gaillac are touring the world. The Plageoles' Vin d'Autan, an exotic, sweet wine, fabulously long in the mouth, is classed among the fifty best wines on the planet!

Au Domaine des Très Cantous, on invente de nouveaux grands vins, sans renier, bien au contraire, l'héritage millénaire du Gaillacois.

A bunch of *mauzac* grapes with their delicate apple flavour in the hands of Robert Plageoles *(above)*.

In this wine cellar, the old vintages covered with dust are much coveted *(right)*.

At Fronton, the revolution began in the eighties. After being successively the vineyard of the Hospitallers of Saint John of Jerusalem – who cleared the immense forest of Agre –, then the supplier of the working class when Fronton was only a large market town, this Haute-Garonne vineyard equipped itself with new barrels, began to refine its vinification and proved that its vine, the *négrette* – associated with syrah and cabernet – could produce great wine. Two huge estates, Bellevue-la-Forêt and Château Montauriol, were at the forefront of this revival, which is currently being given a second wind by young wine growers such as the Ribes brothers. Similarly, the award of appellation contrôlée in 1989 to the tiny vineyard of Marcillac in Aveyron was due to the tal-

When the grapes have been harvested, they are put to ferment in tanks. Pictured here is a traditional concrete tank from the Domaine de Birecap in the Côtes de Gascogne.

ent and the tenacity of winegrowers like Philippe Teulier, of the Domaine du Cros, and Jean-Luc Matha, of Le Vieux Porche. They revived a vineyard which had been planted in the 10th century by the monks of the Abbey of Conques, then decimated by phylloxera, and finally replanted to slake the thirst of the miners of the coal basins of Decazeville, until the mines closed and wine growing took off. Their superbly fleshy and fruity red wines are the ideal accompaniment to local delicacies such as Rouergue tripe and *aligot*.

All the wines of Midi-Pyrénées have been influenced by the driving force of these individuals in the Lot, Gers, Tarn, Haute-Garonne and Aveyron areas and have benefited from their savoir faire and their business acumen. The wine growers of meridional Toulouse, Languedoc and the Pyrenees are conquering European, and even world, markets. An outstanding example of success in this field is that of the Grassas, son and daughter, of Château Tariquet who have a picaresque family background featuring Aragon, Ariège, New York at its most chic and now third generation apprenticeships on the other side of the Atlantic. The style and pugnacity of the Grassa family have brought back nobility, and particularly pride, to the white wines of Gascony which, for a long time, were fit only for distilling.

But quality is not the prerogative of private cellars. The cooperative which links the Plaimont producers for example, supported by the Saint-Mont appellation, directs peasant viniculture towards quality as well as enterprise – they were responsible for a vine planted one night in the Place du Capitole in Toulouse, the Colombelle and the Colombard of Daguin –, and today federates partners from other strongly individual vineyards, such as Marcillac, Fronton and Gaillac. It has even reinvented, at the bottom end of the range, but with all the impudence of chic luxury, "*vin de soif*", sold under this very heading to match both its status and its humanist intentions!

For the vine does not only signify wine: it also represents a multitude of country areas cultivated by wine growers which more and more townsfolk like to visit, make their own and share with their friends. Present fashion is for "durable" development. Well, so much the better: the vine is there in the countryside for generations to come! ■

The superbly fleshy and fruity Marcillac reds are the ideal accompaniment to local delicacies such as Rouergue tripe and *aligot*.

The vineyards are ablaze as harvesting approaches. At Jean-Luc Matha's estate, the harvest is transported by head on sheer hills that tractors refuse to climb.

The *quint-essence*

Claude Posternak
Estate owner
château of Neguebouc
Haut-Armagnac

UNLIKE OTHER WINEGROWERS, those of Armagnac do not seek to achieve a high degree of alcohol. The two ingredients sought after in the Armagnac grape are total acidity and volatile acidity. High total acidity makes it possible to preserve wines without adding any sulphur before distillation. Low volatile acidity, a feature of grapes harvested before maturity without the slightest sign of rot, is the best guarantee of avoiding an over strong ether content. The Armagnac winegrower's efforts are all directed towards this Grail: the exclusion of ether. The principles of distillation have been known since antiquity – the Persians discovered them several

The different Armagnacs are stacked in storehouses where the hydrometry influences the ageing of the alcohol. Pictured here is Benoît Gébert's storehouse at Salles-d'Armagnac *(above)*.

A mobile still, used for Armagnac distillation *(opposite)*.

The distiller has to pick his way through the ethers until he arrives at the "heart", the essence, the fifth element.

centuries before our era – but only reappeared in Europe during the Renaissance. Alchemists discovered at that time that the constituents of a given substance do not vaporise at the same temperature. This meant that one could separate the elements which comprised the grape in order to extract "the most subtle features, which remain once the rough and coarse elements are removed". The distiller has to pick his way between the "heady" ethers - very powerful and flavoursome -, the "secondary" ethers and the "tail" ethers of the final stage of distillation, until he arrives at the "heart", the essence, the essential fifth element.

The Armagnac method of distillation by continuous heating begins ritually every winter in the month of November and continues until February. It is a generous distillation process which enlarges to the maximum the palette of flavours in the distillate. Although it brings out

the qualities of the raw material, it also exaggerates the defects. For it to succeed, the vintage must be perfectly healthy, the wine without the slightest fault. Two thermometers float in the receptacle which holds the distillate as it emerges from the still; one shows the degree of alcohol in the brandy, the other shows the temperature at which it emerges. It actually matters little whether a brandy is between 52 and 55% proof, but it is essential that it should not exceed 15 degrees of temperature otherwise ether content may be excessive… and headaches result! If the temperature has been properly controlled, *folle blanche* wines, which are usually low in alcohol, will make excellent brandies of between 52 and 54% proof, whilst *colombards* will produce balanced distillates of between 56 and 58% proof.

Just as ether should not mask the delicacies of the alcohol, the oak flavour of the barrel should not dominate the flavour of the fruit. It is

Each stage of Armagnac production has its own demands. The winter pruning strengthens the stocks, the heating of the still over wood extracts the different ethers, the storehouse manager measures the degree of the alcohol as it comes out.

there to sublimate it, to add touches of vanilla, cocoa or plum which will complete its olfactory structure. This is why it is important to obtain woods which will add a touch of delicacy. Forests must be chosen where oak trees grow densely, because the more compact the forest – making conditions for the growing tree difficult – the more likely the trunk will be to have a fine grain and less aggressive tannin. It is also important that drying should be done in the open air; a good ten years of exposure to the sun, the rain and the patina of time is a reasonable period. And finally, the heating of the wood as the staves are being assembled must be carried out with respect for the final product; slow, deep heating ensures a future balance between the fruity taste of the alcohol and the

The white alcohol pouring out of the still. A young brandy will register 52° to 65° alcohol. In order to be put on the market, it will have to be brought down progressively to between 40° and 48° by means of ageing in oak barrels.

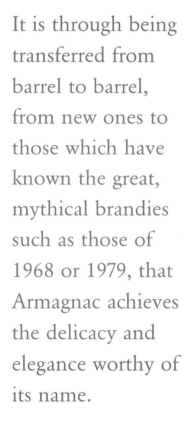

It is through being transferred from barrel to barrel, from new ones to those which have known the great, mythical brandies such as those of 1968 or 1979, that Armagnac achieves the delicacy and elegance worthy of its name.

delicate notes of the wood. Armagnac must be drawn from its barrel in the height of summer, when the warmth helps to aerate the brandy, so that it loses the obtrusive faults of its early days. This is how Armagnac is raised in the land of rugby: the brandy leaves its family barrel to go into a vat where it meets other Armagnacs of its own age and encounters oxygen, alcohol's best friend!

Year by year, through being transferred from one barrel to another, from new ones to those which have known the great, mythical brandies such as those of 1968 or 1979, Armagnac loses its coarseness and achieves the delicacy and elegance worthy of the oldest brandy in the world. ■

TASTING ARMAGNAC

In 1936, Armagnac was attributed an *appellation d'origine contrôlée* which defines three areas of production: Bas-Armagnac, Haut-Armagnac and Ténarèze.

The ritual can be all-absorbing: when the amber liquid encounters the concave wall of your rounded glass; when the alcohol releases fragrances of prune, preserved orange, vanilla, resin or even rosewood. One must always be comfortably settled so as to unhurriedly enjoy its reflections and its gold glint, its limpidity and its brilliance. Then, oh so carefully, one takes the base of the glass between the thumb and the index finger. An imperceptible movement of the wrist produces a slight swirl of the liquid, which caresses the crystal. Perfumes become discernible. A touch of citron. Your other hand, rounded as if to hold a breast, slips delicately beneath the glass sphere. The crystal settles into the hollow of your palm. The alcohol sways, coats the walls of the glass, then forms tears, in which certain people believe they see legs. An important moment this, as the brandy warms in your hand before it even lets you savour its tender burning taste. New fragrances rise to your face, your eyes feel a slight prickling. It is time to drink. A tiny first sip informs your lips. The Armagnac can be judged by its bite. Then a sensation of fullness, without heaviness, invades your mouth. Strength does not exclude richness or creaminess. Swirl it round your mouth, then swallow. And gauge the effect. For one also judges Armagnac on the long memory it leaves in one's mouth.

The signs of a great vintage: brilliance, limpidity and viscosity *(above and opposite)*.

An Armagnac vineyard near Larroque-sur-l'Osse in the appellation region of Ténarèze *(right)*.

Occupying an area straddling western Gers, the southern tip of Lot-et-Garonne and the east of the Landes, "aygue ardente" has become, along with the goose, a gastronomic emblem of Gascony. In all, 15,000 hectares are given over to this brandy. In 1936, Armagnac was attributed an "appellation d'origine contrôlée" which defines three regions of production. Bas-Armagnac or Armagnac noir extends over light "boulbène" soils and tawny sands. The brandies produced here are reputed for their great finesse. The region of Haut-Armagnac or Armagnac blanc is characterised by predominantly limestone soils. Its distilled white wines engender very rare brandies (less than 2% of the overall production or Armagnac) with a delicate, fruity bouquet. Ténarèze, situated to the centre of the appellation zone, is a half-way house with vines cultivated on predominantly clay and limestone soils. Its brandies are usually generous and heady. The vine occupied an important position in Gers as early as the 11th century but no traces of stills have been found before the 14th century. These copper treasures, which used to burn wood but now employ gas more and more often, move around from property to property. When the still arrives in an estate, it is an occasion for owner and friends to get together to celebrate the "flame", the beginning of distillation.

Paths

of creation

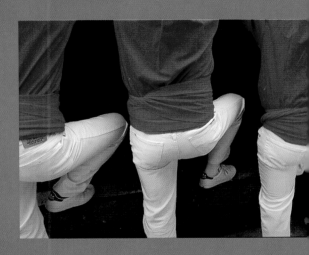

Harmonically yours

Isabelle Deluze
Journalist

QUAI DE LA DAURADE: THE AIR IS WARM and fragrant, as so often on a June day in Toulouse. It is evening, the sounds of the city are dying down. Anna is out walking, enjoying her favourite activity; she breathes in deeply, feeling her ribs stretch out, her body fill out like a sail. She follows the air as it travels through her, exhales sharply. She regulates the intake of air, opening and closing successive, invisible valves that regulate her breathing. She starts again, and smiles. She has not slowed her pace, and her breathing is perfectly regular. She is not out of breath, there is no trace of any unpleasant panting that suggests that the body is weaker than the breathing. Anna controls her breathing perfectly, tuning it as she would a living instrument. Anna is twenty; she is learning singing at the Toulouse conservatoire, or academy of music.

Anna will never forget that audition last September, which opened the doors of the conservatoire. How many of them were there? 150, 200? It was hot, people avoided looking at each other, voices were just that bit too high, everyone waited eagerly and anxiously. At the end of the day, there were ten of them

Young lyric artist, rehearsing at Saint-Pierre-des-Cuisines, Toulouse, in front of an empty auditorium.

Leontina Veduva in *Romeo and Juliet,* at the Capitole, Toulouse *(opposite).*

left. They joined some twenty older students. The director of the academy, Marc Bleuse, warned them of the dangers of being too impatient and attempting to try parts for which their young, fragile voices were as yet unprepared. As for Anna, would she have that charisma onstage, that aura which one associates with great singers? The young woman remembered the director's warning; it had impressed her deeply, but it did not weigh her down. Walking lightly along the quayside, she reflected on the alchemy between the city and its voice. She remembered what she had been reading that afternoon, in Déodat de Séverac's correspondence. This is what the composer, who was born in Saint-Félix-Lauragais, wrote in 1902: "On all sides, on the banks, in the coral-tinted mist that rises from the waves of the river to the glowing roofs, songs and choruses ring out endlessly, as night lulls the city

or Anna, would she have that charisma
age, that aura which one associates with
t singers?

e's music
y has a first-class
on. True, courtois
nd singing first
ed here.

These young women
discover the arcana of
melody under the
guidance of their singing
mistress, Anne Fondeville
(*above*).

to sleep, scattering into the distance rhythms of joy and melancholy[1]." And it had been so for at least nine centuries, since *courtois* poetry and songs had first emerged, in the Midi. The troubadours' musical poetry spread from here to the whole of Europe and put out lasting roots in its home region. Which is why people say that Toulouse sings, and has never stopped singing – except for the odd eclipse.

Georges Canet, who is the great master of ceremonies of Toulouse's international song contest, which was founded in 1954, considers that this contest is in many respects the distant heir of those poetry, musical and singing jousts that first took place in Toulouse in 1324 and are known as "Floral Arts". In forty-four years, the song contest is internationally famed and acts as a first springboard for many young singers, some of whom, like Joé Van Dam and Leontina Vadu-va, have become leading names.

Anna's dream is to hear those voices, nothing more. In the past ten years, since Nicolas Joël took over the management of the Capitole theatre, which is in fact the city's opera house, the greatest singers have been invited to Toulouse. It is hard to get a seat; because the opera's 7,000 season-ticket holders ensures a tight circle of chic music-lovers that makes it difficult for others to get a chance to attend a performance. Now and again, Anna manages to get a flap seat and can thus enjoy the magic that sometimes overwhelms her, as when she discovered Natalie Dessay in Ambroise Thomas's *Hamlet*.

Winter in Toulouse glows with the magic of the Capitole Tuesdays, mid-day recitals that take her into the purple-and-gold of Toulouse's Italian opera. Those recitals enable the city's inhabitants to perpetuate a grassroots, music-loving tradition: a century ago, the Toulouse public made and unmade singers of *bel canto*, bombarding singers it considered mediocre with all kinds of projectiles. Crowds used to gather in the cafés on Capitole Square whenever there was a performance, waiting for the ushers to warn them just before the famous pieces; they would then squeeze into the standing-space at the back of the house, which has since vanished. It was an enthusiastic, exacting public, which noisily demonstrated its approval of talent, a public that knew the repertoire so well that a newspaper, *Le Temps*, wrote in 1933: "They are illiterate workmen, tailors and masons, but they know the most beautiful tunes of Rossini, Weber and Meyerbeer by heart; they sing them with an aplomb and a mastery that would do credit to the best musicians. The opera is their school."

Anna knows that the memory of those famous Toulouse voices, of those tenors who were trained in the local conservatoire, which opened in 1820, is written into the city's history. Here, Merly was born in 1828: he was a magnificent tragedian, a singer whose wide-ranging voice enabled him to sing parts written for baritones as well as tenors. There lived Victor Capoul, who was born in 1839, a tenor beloved of ladies. A century later, other fine voices made their mark too: Mady Mesplé, a soprano, who runs a master class in Aveyron each summer at Sylvanès Abbey; and Jean-Philippe Laffont, a tenor.

The season is packed with so many events that Anna does not know where to turn. The city's symphonic orchestra has built up an international reputation under Michel Plasson's thirty-year baton, and its series of concerts called "Les Grands Interprètes" does just that: bring leading singers, conductors, musicians, orchestras and choirs to the city. Many of these concerts take place at the "Halle aux Grains"

The memory of those famous Toulouse voices who were trained in the local conservatoire, which opened in 1820, is written into the city's history.

In the gold-and-purple Italianate Capitole theatre, *bel canto* and an enthusiastic public *(above and right)*.

Tenor José Van Dam on the stage of the Capitole *(below)*.

Choral singing is very popular in Midi-Pyrénées and counts some 20,000 amateurs.

Déodat de Séverac sang Occitania in many of the works he composed. Here, in the company of friends *(top)*.

Gabriel Fauré, who was born in Pamiers, in Ariège, composed *Penelope*, an opera that has been unfairly forgotten *(above)*.

the former corn exchange, that has become a concert-house. Even so, Anna prefers those smaller, more intimate places, that are wrapped in their own magic. What better place to hear an alto than the delicate Carmélites chapel that is tucked away rue du Périgord? The Red Room, at the Musée des Augustins, was a suitable setting for Montserrat Figueras and Jordi Savall, when they were invited by the association Arts Renaissants. Toulouse's Saint-Sernin basilica, whose nave is illuminated at night, provides an awe-inspiring setting, as on that April evening when she heard a vocal ensemble there, Les Eléments, the only other professional choir in the region besides the Capitole choir, whom Pierre Iodice directs. In Midi-Pyrénées, though, choral singing is very popular and counts some 20,000 amateurs. Only fifty years ago, the only choirs in the region were those of parish churches.

The swift emergence of top-quality amateur choirs is due to the formidable energy and expectations of a petite woman, Alix Bourbon. Besides training singers, she has worked hard to include works by local composers in the repertoire: pieces of folklore music, that have been adapted by Noël Lancien, who directed the conservatoire; a 14th century Toulouse mass; Renaissance works composed by Antoine de Bertrand, Guillaume Boni and de Bouzignac; and, of course, those composed by Déodat de Séverac, even though he did not write much for choirs, by de Dalayrac, who was born in Muret, and a mass by Aymé Kunc who, in the 1940, directed the conservatoire.

Alix Bourbon was a student at the Toulouse academy of music; so was Joël Suhubiette, who conducts Les Eléments. Like Alix Bourbon, he is an enthusiastic champion of first-rate amateur choirs. For thirteen years, Joël Suhubiette was a member of the Chapelle royale and Gand's Collegium Vocale, directed by Philippe Herreweghe, whom he considers his master and worked with as the latter's assistant. And although, since 1990, Joël Suhubiette has been directing the all-professional Chœur de Chambre, he has also been conducting an amateur group, the Ensemble vocal, for the past sixteen years.

Joël Suhubiette is also attached to the region's composers, who are present in his repertoire, favouring contemporary ones. In 1995, he created at Auch *Stabat Mater*, by Patrick Burgan, a Toulousain, and in 1998, he created his *Audi Coelum* for the Toulouse Organ Festival.

Anna is training to become a soloist; many of her friends and fellow students sing in amateur choirs. Some of them have joined the regional choir, Chœur de Toulouse Midi-Pyrénées, directed by François Terrieux, who is their choir master at the conservatoire. One

Top-quality amateur choral singing is widespread in the region: proof of this talent is the excellent Chœur de Toulouse Midi-Pyrénées.

Sunday in June, they gave a concert in Auch cathedral, for the "Éclat de Voix" festival. It was a festival that brought singers together, amateurs and professionals, and various kinds of vocal art, "spoken, sung, whispered, confidential, erotic"… to quote the festival director, Patrick de Chirée.

The Auch festival marked the opening of a dizzy summer festival season throughout Midi-Pyrénées.

Summer really gets going in Lauragais, at Saint-Félix, where Déodat de Séverac was born. His grandson, Gilbert Blacque-Belair revived his grandfather's works and deeply Occitanian outlook some ten years ago. Anna loves those colourful and sophisticated musical pieces that tell of the Midi, of Lauragais and Cerdagne, that provide melodies for Goudouli's poetry, jolt instruments into playing a sardana dance tune and are a general hymn to nature. It is all that which accounts for the captivating magic of the Saint-Félix festival, where concerts take place on the market-square and in the wine-cellars at Ravan, and are rounded off with convivial picnics.

The next stop for Anna is at Pamiers, that still throbs to the memory of Gabriel Fauré, who was born there; at the conservatoire she is working on some of his melodies, *Mandoline, Après un rêve..* Some day, perhaps, she will sing *Penelope*, his unfairly forgotten opera.

Later, in Comminges, round a bend in the road, Anna sees rising before her, against the green slopes of the Pyrenees, the austere mass of Saint-Bertrand-de-Comminges. Concerts there are a powerful experience, especially those for voice and organ, that the Festival du Comminges organises since 1975. The effect is of a mystical, entrancing meeting of souls. During the Festival, an international academy of music brings together trainee singers and musicians from the whole world, who meet there to study singing, organ-playing and musicology. Visitors sometimes come across a music lesson in the small cathedral choir or in the cypress garden behind the nearby cathedral of Saint-Just-de-Valcabrère: a rendezvous of music, summer heat and good humour.

During the summer, Anna travels to Rouergue, to a shaded valley where Sylvanès Abbey nestles. It is a place where the wind, the birds, everything is conducive to spiritual meditation, to the communion of voice and nature. Father André Gouze, a Dominican, has devoted much of his life to Sylvanès, which he first restored, cleaning th

Sylvanès now plays host to the most important festival of sacred music in Midi-Pyrénées; since 1990, it also houses Michel Piquemal's European Academy of Choirs and Orchestras.

August takes Anna along the byways of Lot, to the Saint-Céré festival, which Olivers Desbordes has been directing since 1980. The atmosphere there is unique: productions are staged in marvellous settings such as Castelnau's ruined castle, Souillac's Romanesque abbey, Carennac's cloister.

"Eclats de Voix", the Auch festival, that celebrated all kinds of vocal art, "spoken, sung, whispered, confidential, erotic"…

Every production conveys an infinite creative freedom that captivates Anna. An Arab-Andalusian *Carmen* created in Marrakech the previous spring had an electrifying effect on the public that had gathered in Lot that summer. Georges Bizet's opera has been boldly attuned to Moroccan music; western and Arab instruments share the score. Saint-Céré offers singers parts they will never find elsewhere, parts that are conceived as a hand outstretched to the widest-possible public. That is why, in the winter, Georges Desbordes and his company, l'Opéra Eclaté, travel up and down the country with their instruments and adjustable sets, performing in villages and small towns.

This open-minded, open-hearted attitude sets Anna thinking about her future career and duty to society as a singer…

September has come. Anna is back in Toulouse with her friends. They arrange to meet at the Jacobins cloister, and settle between the hedges of scented boxwood to hear the best pianists in the world, who have been invited to "Piano aux Jacobins". A chic public is seated in the chapter-house. Students from the neighbouring Lycée Fermat listen at the windows. The summer tempo melodiously glides into the harmonics of autumn.

Back at the conservatoire, Anna starts working again under her singing-mistress, Anne Fondeville, throbbing with new sensations, ready for more musical experiences and the thrills they promise. ■

The autumn season opens with "Piano aux Jacobins", which brings together world-famous pianists in the arcaded cloister *(above)*.

Pleasures of the boards

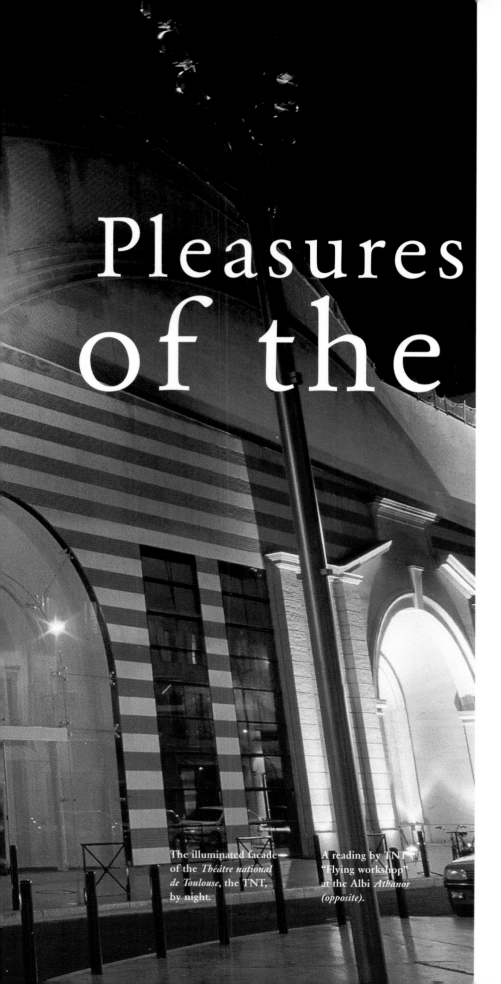

The illuminated façade of the *Théâtre national de Toulouse*, the TNT, by night.

A reading by TNT's "Flying workshop" at the Albi *Athanor* (*opposite*).

Pierre Bruel
Theatre critic

Let's set the scene.

For too long, far too long, complaining spirits could grumble that Midi-Pyrénées was a cultural desert as regards the theatre. On the day of his twentieth birthday, Maurice Sarrazin, together with Simone Turck, founded the Grenier in Toulouse. Just after the war the terrain was thus occupied by the Turcks and Sarrazins… At first, the Grenier had no regular premises and simply toured the area until, in 1964, the Sorano Theatre was created. More recently, new venues have been established throughout Midi-Pyrénées. When Rosner succeeded Sarrazin there was a general clear-out. Rosner left

It is not just the actors who play their part, the spectators also play the game, enjoying themselves and listening to a language which is so different from what they hear every day.

Toulouse once he had achieved his ambition of establishing the Théâtre National de Toulouse in France's fourth city. This huge entity is directed by Jacques Nichet, who was born in Albi and is an ardent defender of poetry in all its forms. Just get an eyeful of the programme…

But let's leave the beaten track.

What is in this word "theatre"? On first contact the theatre is something that you feel, something that gets you in the guts. Above all it is for playing: it is not just the actors who play their part, the spectators also play the game, enjoying themselves and listening to a language which is so different from what they hear every day, whether it is the language of the music hall or a more elevated kind.

Today's experiments should prepare the ground for tomorrow's

theatre, and on this score one might quote *"Urgence de la jeune parole"* organised by the Digue Theatre, in which young actors were working with teenagers. There are also the Gueuloirs operations with the Fédération nationale des companies de théâtre (FNCTA): the indefatigable Didier Albert, in his Théâtre de Poche, brings rough texts out of storage and into the open.

Theatre is visual pleasure. It is the extreme beauty of the natural site of the Cirque de Gavarnie; it is the Cathedral at Rodez with its square (in which *Fleur de vie* was created) and its steeple ("the most beautiful steeple in France" according to Chateaubriand) which was illuminated by Jacques Rouveyrollis for Antoine Colinet; it is all the artistic sites (and they are legion) which are the patrimony of Midi-Pyrénées, transformed by structures and scenery originally taken from *l'Arche de Noé* (Noah's Ark); it is the Cornet à Dés, which displayed the

Absorbed in their work: director Maurice Sarrazin and actor Daniel Sorano. The Toulouse *Grenier*, initially an itinerant troupe, obtained a permanent theatre, the *Sorano*, in 1964. It has since become one of Toulouse's institutions.

La Mer by Édouard Bond, directed by Jacques Rosner *(second from left)*.

The actor Philippe Torreton being made up in preparation for Shakespeare's *Henry V*.
Le Phun in *Les Cent Dessous*, a piece of street theatre.

The festival of Vaour is the pleasure of pure laughter, without sound track or canned laughter.

paintings of Jérôme Bosch, and the Oeil du silence at Anglars in the Lot area; it is all the décors bearing the hallmark of their stage designers, including that of *Comment va le monde, Monsieur?* which completely took over the stage at Odyssud; it is the "Théâtre d'images", the Caroube, the Marionnettissimo festival, the creations of the Tatoo Theatre…

Theatre is emotion which goes straight to your heart. The Comédiens au Chariot criss-crossing Rouergue at the time of Concorde

An open air performance in period costumes holds this Lot audience spellbound as night descends over the Château de Cazals *(above)*.

An actor contemplating the geometric scenery for Aeschylus's *Persians*, directed by Olivier Werner *(opposite)*.

with their horse-drawn wagon; all those places imbued with the soul of their creator – the Cave Po', the Pavé, the Apollo at Mazamet: it would be nice to cast a spotlight on each of them, not forgetting the Parvis at Tarbes-Ibos, which has proved that theatres and hypermarkets can make an excellent combination.

Theatre is the pleasure of pure laughter, without sound track or canned laughter. In Tarn, there is the festival of Vaour, and in Toulouse, the *Printemps des courges* rechristened *Printemps du rire*. The theatre can stimulate your zygomatic muscles and your neurones. Today there is so much choice – one chapter cannot nearly do justice to the subject.

If you have the opportunity, treat yourself to the privilege of watching a rehearsal. Or attend the improvisation sessions given by the master of this art: Jean-Pierre Tailhade.

The Cahors theatre has succeeded in gaining the allegiance of an audience appreciative of contemporary creation *(top)*.

This actor is proud of having been designated the future successor to Feruccio Soleri, who has been playing the role of Harlequin in Carlo Goldoni's Arlecchino since 1956 *(above)*.

Theatre is the thrill of all those evenings spent listening to penetrating scripts. Evenings when the spectator emerges feeling a little wiser.

Theatre can be the pleasure of a discovery: finding a former pupil of the Toulouse Conservatoire, Roger Louret, bringing his play *J'ai vingt ans et je m'emmerde* to the Sorano, with, as its interpreter, an unknown but brilliant young actress who was already setting the boards alight: Muriel Robin.

Theatre can be the pleasure of a surprise: Jean Bousquet in *Ce soir on improvise,* improvising "for real" with a spectator who was provoking him in the foyer of the Sorano. An unexpected pleasure for one and all. Or the joy of witnessing the moment when an actor suddenly assumes the character of the role he is playing. If you have the opportunity, treat yourself to the privilege of watching a real rehearsal. Attend some improvisation competitions ("Enjoy something you'll never see twice") organised by groups like C Cédille, or one of the improvisation sessions given in public by the man who remains the master of this art: Jean-Pierre Tailhade.

Theatre can be the pleasure of innovation, of new trends, the programmes of the Garonne or Balatum Theatres or even TG Stan…

Theatre is those performances that live in your memory, like the first time the Piccolo Teatro de Milano put on *Arlechino servitore di due padroni* in the Capitole in the early sixties. Ferruccio Soleri, who has taken the role of Harlequin since 1956, has played this part at the Sorano, at the TNT, in the Parvis at Tarbes, and at Odyssud.

Vis-à-vis brings a fresh look to the circus by flirting with poetry, dance and theatre. Here Lionel About is pictured in *Visa pour l'amour.*

217

Theatre is the pleasure of watching enthusiastic young troupes.

I wish you the enjoyment of those special evenings when the delighted spectator, overwhelmed with happiness, takes hours to come back to earth. Recreation/re-creation, and a lot more besides... This mysterious pleasure is part and parcel of the spectacle of course, but also of you.

So move along, there's plenty to see.

I wish you the pleasure of participating in truly "animated" performances. To take one example out of a thousand, just cross the threshold of the Barraca and let the Didier Carette atmosphere seize you. Is it the filtered lighting; the décor which is changed every season; the music, now joyful, now nostalgic? Is it the first reception room (sorry, "welcoming room"), where host receives guest; the drawn curtain

From left to right:
Scene from a performance of *Arlecchino servitore di due padroni* **given by the** *Piccolo Teatro* **of Milan.**

Casimir and Caroline, **by Ödön von Horwáth, the story of an impossible love, directed by Jacques Nichet, artistic director at TNT.**

In Midi-Pyrénées, two complementary approaches to the cinema cohabit. One emphasises the importance of the audio-visual heritage and is embodied in the Toulouse Cinémathèque which, presided over by Daniel Toscan du Plantier, is second only to Paris in terms of the scope of its collection. The other concentrates on the future of the cinematic industry with more and more major productions being filmed in the area. André Téchiné, a native of Valence-Agen, chose Toulouse for his intimate film Ma saison préférée, presented at Cannes in 1993, but it was the success in 1995 of Le bonheur est dans le pré by Étienne Chatiliez, set in the Gers countryside, which turned the spotlight on the region. The same year, the introductory sequence to the new James Bond film, Goldeneye, was filmed in Peyragudes, in the Pyrenees, and the latter also served as a backdrop to one of French cinema's most recent successes, Le Pacte des loups. Un amour d'enfance, a first film from director Yves Caumon, a native of Tarn, was acclaimed in the "Un certain regard" category of the Cannes Film Festival. Several festivals contribute to boosting the vitality of the seventh art in Midi-Pyrénées: the Cinespaña festival devoted to Spanish cinema and the Rencontres of Latin American cinema, in Toulouse; the Rencontres at Gindou in Lot, dedicated to the cinema of black Africa and the Mediterranean, and the Résistances festival at Foix in Ariège, known for its alternative cinema.

I wish you the enjoyment of those special evenings when the delighted spectator, overwhelmed with happiness, takes hours to come back to earth.

which conceals the auditorium – are we about to enter a circus ring? In the obscurity you sit in candle light behind school kids' desks, or on an old red theatre chair, heavy with memories... waiting to receive a beverage, a theatrical love potion.

The play begins, although the spectacle has already begun! Within strange scenery, made from bits of timber salvaged from *The Master and Marguerita*, the actors say their lines which the director has skilfully tailored. You may see that the actors are speaking their words with the text in their hands.

Plays change each week: no-one can work miracles! These actors, accomplices in the drama, live their role before you, for you, with you and with such fervour that you are no longer aware that they are reading from paper. Actually I don't think they are reading – of course they check that the lines they have just "improvised" for you were what they were meant to say. This evening the god of the theatre is with them. And also with you.

Another type of spectacle which is very much alive comes under the heading "arts of the street, arts of the ring". Is this a new kind of circus, or new theatre? Since the departure of the famous Troupe Royale de Luxe, the artistic initiative has moved from Toulouse to surrounding areas. It is in Auch, with its Circa festival; in Ramonville, with its festival of street theatre; in Saint-Orens, with its Nez Rouges festival; with the Pronomades troupe set up by Philippe Saunier-Borrel which play in several towns in Haute-Garonne...

We'll leave the final word to Laure Nusset. Writing in *Intra Muros* about the youthful Compagnie 111, she said: "It is hardly an exaggeration to say that Toulouse is the breeding ground of the new circus. The Lido, centre of circus arts in Toulouse, has produced a considerable number of the jugglers and clowns now on the world scene – an achievement of which we are justly proud. Vis-à-vis, Vent d'Autan and the Acrostiches represent a resurgence of those types of circus which flirt with poetry, dance and theatre."

Clear the floor: everyone on stage! ∎

A costumed actress, on her way from her dressing room to the stage of TNT.

Pascal Alquier

Journalist

A mix of voices and races

THE SONGS OF THE TROUBADOURS still resonate in the minds of Midi-Pyrénées performing artists. It is as though, handed down from time immemorial, accents and rhythms drawn from Occitan culture still vibrate in the veins of the Nougaros and other local interpreters. The "*petit taureau*" of the Minimes surely refers, however innocently, to the Catharist poets, praising their inspiration and their attachment to a land which had nourished them, body and soul. When Magyd Cherfi of the group Zebda evokes his "*Toulousain*-ness", he quite simply confirms the region as a melting pot of races, sounds and senses, whose influences are drawn from all around the Mediterranean basin, including of course neighbouring Spain. The flamenco guitarist Bernardo Sandoval (who received a César in 1998 for best film music for *Western* by Manuel Poirier) continues with astonishing elegance the tradition of "Spanish blues" as defined by Miles Davis. He occupies a prominent place in a generation of Spanish immigrants that proudly

Toulouse's *enfants terribles*, Zebda, are presently top of the bill. Here pictured at the Zénith, the leading venue in the *Ville rose*.

Magyd Cherfi, whose voice is Zebda's calling card *(opposite)*.

bears the torch of flamenco. Others include Vicente, son of the famous dancer, Isobel Soler, and the painter, Carlos Pradal, who, as befits his personal history, interprets the work of Spanish poets on the national and international scene. Antonio "Kiko" Ruiz (first prize for guitar at Toulouse's Casa España in 1977 and first prize for flamenco guitar in the 1990 Nimes international competition) has also taken part in this resurgence of flamenco for which our region can be justly proud. Even La Joselito - the doyenne of flamenco - celebrates his authenticity and purity of style. Together with others like the tenor Ruben Velasquez, the Femmouzes T and, of course, the Fabulous Trobadors, they are the very incarnation of that secret alchemy by which the art of the troubadours is skilfully blended with a modern idiom acknowledged by a public avid for new musical sensations. This region, more than anywhere

Bernardo Sandoval, Ruben Velasquez, Les Femmouzes T… This region, more than anywhere else, has provided a breeding ground for the mixture of cultures and voices to flourish.

The "Alors… Chante!" festival at Montauban, devoted to French-speaking performers, uncovers new talents each year *(above)*.

Les Fabulous Trobadors *(right)* opened the way to a kind of "Occitan rap", later taken up, notably, by Les Femmouzes T.

else, has provided a breeding ground for the mixture of cultures and voices to flourish through the ages. Indeed for centuries past, the registers of the music societies and academies in our region have been proof of the existence and melodic fertility of exceptionally talented musicians and singers. Peire Vidal (1165-1205), one of the most prominent troubadours, was in the service of Raimon V at Toulouse. Uc Brunet and Lo Com worked at Rodez at the same time, and it was in 1322 that the Gay Savoir company (which became the Académie des Jeux Floraux) was formed on the initiative of seven minstrels. In the 17th century the Languedoc poet Goudouli, who is commemorated in Place Wilson in Toulouse, was awarded the "*fleur du souci*" by the Jeux Floraux for his *Chant Royal*. His works travelled all over the world.

The names of Jelyotte (first singer in the *Opéra du Roi* in the middle of the 18th century) and the tenors Gayé and Victor Capoul

Art Mengo, Statics
and Bernardo
Sandoval – all
local vocalists.
Claude Nougaro
could be said to
be their spiritual
father.

marked their period. The latter became Director of the New York Conservatory, then returned to the *Opéra de Paris*. Their talent, the quality of their voices and their presence enabled them to stand out in roles usually reserved for Parisians who happened to be in favour but, after winning the hearts of the public in the regional capital, they were prepared for whatever challenge. This was the golden age of bel canto, of which Pierre Nougaro, Claude Nougaro's father, was one of the last great exponents.

But the most famous of Toulouse's offspring was, without doubt, Charles Romuald Gardes, born on the 11th December 1890 and better known under the name Carlos Gardel. He lived in Toulouse for three years as a boy, in the Rue du Canon d'Arcole, where a commemorative plaque carries his name (a stele in memory of this illustrious local child is in the nearby Compans park). He then went to Argentina where to this day he is still literally worshipped. Inventor of the sung tango, his dazzling career has left its mark for ever in the hearts of enthusiastic aficionados. In his early days, the artist interpreted music from the Argentinean countryside, only coming to the tango later. But, could it be the brief influence of "Midi-Pyrénées" melodies or a confirmation of the universal art of the troubadours? No doubt a combination of the two. However it was, the young Gardel, following the example of the Argentinean *payadores* (itinerant troubadours of the 19th century who, travelling in the wake of wagons making their way across the country towards Buenos Aires, gave the tango its true credentials), forged his style as musicians had done in the Middle Ages, basing himself on an oral tradition.

And even though here manners are rough and ready, "*on se traite de con à peine qu'on se traite*" as Nougaro put it, the spirit of celebration and tolerance is predominant, as witness the Convivencia festival. The heart and soul of this festival is a barge, *Chèvrefeuille*, situated at Ramonville-Saint-Agne, which, to the accompaniment of melodies of multiple origins, links the two seas by means of the Canal du Midi. Convivencia, living together, was a key word in the days of the troubadours and has its equivalent in French, Italian, Catalan, Castillian and Portuguese. The festival "*Alors…Chante!*" devoted to French songs, which takes place annually at Montauban, provides the opportunity for a real meeting between the public on the one hand and established or unknown artistes on the other.

The Toulouse Zénith. Futurist architecture for this new venue dedicated to music in Midi-Pyrénées *(above)*.

Realistic songs have found in Jehan a performer of rare sensitivity *(below)*.

> The group Zebda are an incarnation of the easy communication and bonhomie of the south-west. Their humanist messages are in tune with an open-minded and tolerant youth.

Of course there's no need to force nature in this regard; a live current already runs between stage and audience. If we bring to mind the careers of Gold, Images, Richard and Daniel Seff, Jean-Pierre Mader, Pauline Ester, Art Mengo, Serge Guirao, Fly and the Tox, who emerged in the eighties, we can appreciated how attached they have all been to our region. Most of them remain rooted in the Midi-Pyrénées, cherishing this *"torrent of stones"* which characterises our accent, and taking advantage of the professional facilities which exist here: the Polygone studios of Blagnac regularly receive performers of international standing. And although in 1987 Claude Nougaro chose to record his comeback album in New York *(Nougayork)*, he returned to the banks of the Garonne in 1989 for his following disk *(Pacifique)*, mixed in part at Polygone. The son of a baritone and pianist, brought up on airs by Massenet, Puccini and Fauré, Nougaro has been a permanent feature of French music from the mid fifties on. Pearls like *Le Jazz et le Java*, *Bidonville*, *Armstrong*, *Tu verras*, *C'est une Garonne*, *Toi là-haut* and *Toulouse* are landmarks in his work, which is now recognised as equal to that of the most talented poets of our time.

The eighties saw a pause in the succession of hits originating in our region, but inspiration was subsequently renewed and the late nineties saw the arrival of a new crop of artistes with styles as varied as those of Juliette, Moos and Zebda.

The latter, a group of seven coming from the north of Toulouse (Golden Disk for *Essence ordinaire*; two *Victoires de la Musique* in 2000) are in themselves an incarnation of the easy communication and bonhomie of the south-west. Pieces celebrating laughter and fun, as well as humanist and political messages, find in them ideal composer-interpreters, in tune with an open-minded and tolerant youth.

Presently at the summit of their fame, they are being succeeded by a new wave of performers of all styles, from festive rock to realistic songs, as well as pop and rap: Spook and the Guay, 100% Collègues (which contains certain members of Zebda as well as other talented musicians such as Jean-Luc Amestoy, Serge Lopez, Marc Dechaumont, Pascal Rollando, Philippe Dutheil and Bernardo Sandoval), KDD, My Favourite Dentist is Dead, Véro Ségo, Statics and Beautés Vulgaires. Although less in the limelight, the careers of Jehan, Éric Lareine, Georges Baux (pianist-arranger to Bernard Lavilliers amongst others) and Alain Leprest nevertheless deserve special attention because of their engaging and original personalities. This veritable reservoir of talent helps in establishing Midi-Pyrénées as an area of musical experimentation in perpetual movement. ■

CARLOS GARDEL

Éric Lareine, singer-songwriter. An outstanding performer, his husky voice seems to reach deep into the soul *(below)*.

Born in Toulouse in 1890, Charles Romuald Gardes, better known as Carlos Gardel, was the inventor of the sung tango *(above)*.

Juliette, a singular artiste, who appeared in a wave of new talent in the 90s *(below)*.

JAZZ: FULL OF SOUND AND FURY

The glorious thirties were a milestone in the history of the genre. At that time there were countless famous clubs or haunts where big bands and celebrated jazzmen performed. Even though the situation is radically different today (Toulouse, for example, now only has the Mandala as a jazz venue, carefully nurtured by Jean Cartini), a plethora of musicians has distinguished the local jazz scene: Richard Calléja, Pierre Boussaguet, Akim Bournane, Guy Lafitte, the Tuxedo Big Band, Christian "Tonton" Salut and Magali Pietri, to name but a few. The eighties were also a landmark in history, as a multitude of venues devoted to jazz

A trumpeter originating from New Orleans, Wynton Marsalis was the wonder of the 80s integrating many different jazz styles *(above)*.

Oscar Peterson, virtuoso pianist: another of those who has made the journey to Gers *(below)*.

Maceo Parker. With his outfit he carries on the big band tradition in his own jazz-funk style *(centre)*.

Al Grey, the American trombonist, has played with the greats *(below)*.

The great jazz musicians have all been to Marciac: Ray Charles, Tito Puente, Michel Petrucciani … The trumpeter Wynton Marsalis returns each year.

were opened, leading on to the establishment of prestigious festivals. "Le mai du Jazz" at Toulouse prefigured "Jazz sur son 31"; and then there were also "Jazz'velanet" at Lavelanet in Ariège, "Jazz Balade" in Tarn, "Souillac en Jazz", "Millau en Jazz", "Jazz à Montauban", "Jazz à Luz" and in particular the huge festival at Marciac which assembles the cream of the jazz scene in the height of the summer, around bottles of good wine and food lovingly concocted according to the traditional cuisine of the south-west. This recognition on the part of the artistic world is due largely to the efforts of Guy Lafitte and Jean-Louis Guilhaumon, who have managed to forge close bonds with the leading lights of world jazz. The greatest of the great have come to Marciac: Ray Charles, Herbie Hancock, Eddie Palmieri, Tito Puente, Dave Holland, Michel Petrucciani, Pat Metheny...; the trumpeter Wynton Marsalis found the Gers area so welcoming and so uniquely peaceful on his first visit that he makes a point of coming back year after year.

Jazz in Marciac, twenty years of programming that has brought together living legends – here Ray Charles and Dee Dee Bridgewater – and up and coming performers – Ray Baretto and Wynton Marsalis.

Work
in progre

D
A

TIMES ARE CHANGING, FORTUNATELY. Paris
only place in France where artists can
name for themselves, or where art-lovers can
artistic trends and add to their collections whe
both the intellectual and financial ability
change, however, did not come about alone.
nacy of enlightened art-dealers and devoted p
to reverse a trend that was largely due to the
spread by the art-lovers' milieu, which was o
preen itself before the narcissic mirror of a s
to their vanity, as Baudelaire had already n
19th century. As for the artists, they needed
falls, an impression of failure if for some
failed to "go up" to Paris, and the dangers o

Big retrospective of Pierre
Soulages' *Œuvre au noir*,
at the Abattoirs,
Toulouse's Museum of
Modern Art

Victor Gray, one of the
pioneers of abstraction in
Midi-Pyrénées *(opposite)*

Albi's Berbie Palace:
Toulouse-Lautrec's
hometown houses the
world's biggest collection
of his works *(opposite)*.

The female body
fascinates Bernard
Dufour, who works and
lives on the border of Lot
and Aveyron *(below)*.

conventionality and academic stiltedness of provincial art. Through their work and personal determination, they had to prove that one could live "en province", in our region, and still be creative. So doing, they have reversed the trend and made it possible for those who had been drawn into the centripetal Parisian art-world to return to Midi-Pyrénées, besides encouraging artists from other regions to settle here too, and enjoy excellent working conditions in a creative atmosphere.

What is striking about contemporary art in Midi-Pyrénées is its extraordinary diversity and the wealth of artistic resources that are avail-

Works by Delacroix,
Manet, Rubens, on
show at the Musée des
Augustins, Toulouse,
which also houses
a fine collection of
Romanesque art *(below)*.

able in the region as a whole: all the schools of research and inventiveness that stimulate French, but also European and even world art are present here. Whatever scale of values one may choose to attribute to men and works of art, they represent a palette of artistic creativity that places Midi-Pyrénées in an enviable position, and enables the region to emulate the world's leading art centres. Except for instances of regional, passé, art-forms, that one finds elsewhere, artistic production in Midi-Pyrénées, far from being provincial, is a dynamic, living art attuned to its province.

For, even while it belongs to the international mainstreams of contemporary creativity, the art production of Midi-Pyrénées reflects its own specific originality. This is not due to the emergence of some regional idiosyncrasy, that could be linked to the Occitan revival, or to

result of a melting-point of individual and collective characteristics that make for historically objective realities. Midi-Pyrénées is a welding of Languedoc and Gascony, two former historical entities that each gave rise to rich cultural traditions and decisively contributed to shape France's national identity. Their history has shaped the image of our region, an image that should continue to evolve as a result of a constant creativity that is inherent to its art and to its ability to fashion an original cultural context.

The region's older artists, Pierre Soulages, Olivier Debré, Michel Carrade, Pierre Igon, Bernard Dufour, André Marfaing, Félix Denax, were born here or chose to settle here. Their works distil a movingly austere, spiritual vigour, that leaps off plane surfaces and is worked with traditional chromatic materials or an elemental use of clay, thereby joining up with the style of Spanish contemporary artists such as Millares and Tàpies, and Italians like Fontana and Burri. The way in which these various Mediterranean artists have moved and worked in similar directions suggests that a given historical context is in fact the result of a collective effort, in which each and every artist contributes to give shape to something that can only occur in a given part of the world and not elsewhere.

These trends are currently explored, taken up or challenged by a new, restless and demanding generation of artists, who include Juan Jordà, Claude Jeanmart, Michel Fourcade and Michel Cure. Each in his way, following his own mood, has either been receptive to an effusion

Artistic production in Midi-Pyrénées, far from being provincial, is a dynamic, living art attuned to its province.

Hôtel d'Assezat, Toulouse, a Renaissance shrine to house the gems of the Bamberg Foundation, which centres on Bonnard and the Nabis *(top left)*.

Bourdelle's sculptures, at the Musée Ingres, Montauban *(opposite)*.

Spanish painter Juan Jordà has brought expressionism to the artistic scene of Midi-Pyrénées *(above)*.

of colour or preferred ascetically austere planes. Through their works one recognises, albeit constantly renewed, an age-long pictorial tradition that is drawn to plane surfaces which suggest light and the spatial infinity of an all-embracing gaze.

If one considers the current rediscovery of figurative art and technically innovative art-forms, one recognises an indirect tribute to old imitative traditions which have been unexpectedly updated. Breakthroughs in photography, new computer, numeric and digital technologies combine with the contributions of hyper-realism, pop art and minimalism. Moreover, the individual is presented as participating in the creative process in novel ways, be it in physical and even sexual aspects, featuring as host and creator of a world that one either respects

Through their works one recognises, albeit constantly renewed, an age-long pictorial tradition.

as a work of art or reworks as a fabric of collective and individual experience. Several other trends show an endless capacity on the part of artists in Midi-Pyrénées to push back still further the restless quest of contemporary art; several have opted to rework various currents of surrealism, which have always been a source of fascination here, postdadaism, postmodernism and the artistic potential of hi-tech.

Painting, sculpture, the organisation of space and structuring of bodies consequently combine in new creative approaches to bear fruits that may prove as lasting as those that are already part of our collective heritage, or short-lived experiments that, in spite of their ephemeral nature, indelibly mark a period. Art thus acts as an essential leaven and fashioner of history and life, of reality and the invention of a reality which it represents.

Alain Josseau starts off from painting, to which he returns via the challenge posed by modern technology *(above, left).*

The work of Michel Cure blends sensibility and austerity *(above, right).*

Carlos Pradal, Jacques Brianti, Claude Chaigneau, Don Pablo, members of the Mix-Art group, Jean-Paul Héraud, Rolino Gaspari, Philippe Lamy, Jean-Luc Poivret, Daniel Coulet, Corinne Sentou, Bertrand Meyer-Himhoff, Alain Josseau: there are hundreds of others, highly-talented, old and young, but these are just a few of the names that convey the great diversity of sensibilities and trends; they give an idea of the astonishing range of creativity in our region, that has attracted an increasingly varied public thanks to the success of public and private institutions, which have seen the day in recent years, thanks also to galleries, collective projects and fringe movements, which try to open up the world of art.

As a curator, I have had the opportunity to appreciate again and again the extent to which the strength and creative vigour of Toulouse

Beaulieu Abbey, at Ginals, Tarn-et-Garonne, shelters the modern art collection of the Bonnefoy Foundation *(above).*

Cante rondo leaps off this canvas by Carlos Pradal, who strives to capture instantaneity. A museum at Castres is centred on Spanish art *(opposite).*

Daniel Coulet is both sculptor and painter. He structures space in graphic filigree-work that makes for volume *(far right).*

and its region, in the Middle Ages as in the Modern era, are due to the fact that this part of France has known how to welcome, alongside those who were born here, artists who came from all over the world. This was made possible by the fact that all the necessary economic and cultural conditions existed here, to foster creativity; and this creativity in turn has helped to shape our region.

Hence Midi-Pyrénées' dynamism and potential for creating, spreading and enjoying works of art that is definitely not provincial. ■

Feria in the afternoon

Jean-Pierre Delbouys
Writer

In his dancing slippers, the matador falls in step with the bull, for a fatal tango.

In the low evening sun, with its elongated shadows, the bull's horns are more threatening than ever *(opposite)*.

Some people manage their lives, as best they can; others watch them go by. I have chosen to give mine a rhythm, that interweaves two tempos: bullfighting and rugby.

Powerful rituals scan the year for me, important dates that regulate the seasons: Paris and the kick-off of the Five Nations' Tournament; Easter at Arles; the championship finals; the Feria at Vic; Céret, with its bulls and sardanas; and, to close the season, an end-of-*temporada* rendez-vous in Bayonne, Saragossa or Nîmes, for the vintage feria.

One event I never miss is Vic's Whitsun Feria, perhaps because it is the most feverishly stimulating of them all, the one that is most deeply anchored in the culture of the south-west and means most to me in terms of friendships and satisfactions.

I always set off from Toulouse in the same way, wrapped in the rich magic of Roy Hargrove's trumpet and delicate smoke of an Arturo Fuente Havana. The alchemy of passions that drive me to Vic is something that I refuse to alter: even the sun, miraculously, is

Whitsun at Vic-Fezensac. Thousands of *aficionados* hang on Zotoluco's cape as he begins a regal *faena*.

SERVICE PISTE

LA MONTERA GIMONTOISE

PEÑA LA SUERTE
CLUB TAURIN PAUL RICARD LE HOUGA

always there, year after year, escorting us or welcoming us on arrival. The season, too, is just right. At Whitsun, the wheat is ripening and, beyond Auch, the Gers landscapes are reminiscent of Tuscany. Just before Saint-Jean-Poutge, a field by the road is fringed with the deep red of poppies, that glow like the flash of a cape laid out in the sun for some absent *novillero*.

Time slows down after L'Isle-Jourdain, where I always stop for a coffee in a café under the brick arcades of the main square. From L'Isle to Vic, the smoke of my cigar becomes my hour-glass: its last rings fade away as I start down the winding drive to Vic. This leisureliness is part of the ritual, a moment of solitariness when pictures and memories, some painful, others glowing with hope, rise unhindered, like vulnerable migratory birds that head for familiar lands. This unconstrained

Just before Saint-Jean-Poutge, a field is fringed with the deep red of poppies, that glow like the flash of a cape laid out in the sun for some absent *novillero*…

mental rambling between the sky and hills of Gascony is at once mystical and physical, a sensual, persistent hungering after life.

One does not just plunge into the Feria; one enters the fiesta by degrees, according to preordained rules, by walking in the streets of Vic, meeting up at *La Maison bleue* and the *Curro Romero* and *Querencia* bodegas, in a well-trod circuit where revellers join up with those who have made the Vic Feria what it is: Jean Fitte, Jean-Jacques Baylac, Dédé Cabanne, Marcel Garzelli. Intense feelings heighten those bull-and-rugby gatherings – the Feria coincides with the championship finals in France.

In the night, fans sway down the narrow streets of Vic, while sitting together over a drink, happy to be together once again, we reinvent the world of rugby as eagerly and surely as we rewrite the fate of the bulls we have seen in the arena.

Bare-chested, with only his squire to help him, Richard Milian, nicknamed the "risk-taking toreador", as he dresses in his suit of lights.

Captured by the camera in a moment of intense concentration and remoteness that is rarely disturbed.

No words are exchanged during the photography session. At the end, the bullfighter's face closes. The arena is not far…

The age and weight of the bulls are written on a board, below the breeders' emblems *(above)*.

From the seats in the sun *(sol)*, white handkerchiefs are waved in enthusiasm, against a sea of red bérets and white boaters *(right)*.

Musical bands give the feria its restless tempo, until the musicians finally collapse… *(below)*.

Vic's bullring has its vivid, historic episodes, that dominate other events of the Feria like the peaks of the Pyrenees above a September mist. We have had Ruiz Miguel's *despedida*, Garapito, Palha's famous bull, which charged again and again under the pique until he had driven the caparisoned horses right back, like so many old and faded toys of red and gold. There has been Enrique Ponce's slow trinchera, which fought in the rain against a tough, complex bull who behaved like some devious Ariégeois prop forward. There was a miraculous, dantesque *faena* by Oscar Higares, an intermittent and often inconsistent bullfighter, who took up his sword again at the end of a nightmarish afternoon, in an arena drenched in water and fear. We have seen Barcial's *novillos* dashing out of the toril like young men

who, breaking free at last of their childhood circle of fears, discover that they possess a supernatural vigour.

Those glorious moments are what one expects of a visit to Vic, but the Feria's charm lies elsewhere, too, in those quiet, unassuming miracles that bloom when and where you least expect them, and wait to be gathered like clusters of asphodels that might suddenly grow in the macadam of our cities and lives, invisible to the average passer-by. *Curro Romero*, the bodega, is one of those magical places. Situated in a dark, winding street, it welcomes everyone in. No-one ever pays: you eat, you drink, and you just pop what you want in the slot of a quaint moneybox. The place throbs with the enthusiasm of *aficionados* and the quaint atmosphere of a Gascony Seville. Very late one night, I saw

At *Querencia*, one of the bodegas, *aficionados* go over the afternoon bullfight, their hearts and glasses overbrimming with the feria's joyous liquor.

Night falls over the streets of Vic, the *tariquet* has a golden, mellow flavour, one is simply happy to be there, enjoying the simple, untrammelled joys of life.

All over town, one sees improvised parties of amateurs and professionals jointly dancing sevillanas *(above)*.

Every year, the band from Toulouse's Art Academy joins the fun at Vic *(opposite)*.

the owner of the bodega, under the illusion that he was Curro Romero, no less, tease unsubstantial bulls with a dream *muleta*, with the careful deliberation of myopic inspiration. One night, I drank and shared tapas with the old *peon* of an Andalusian *novillero*; he told me all about his messy life, and his failure to make it to become a bullfighter. As we watched, he stood up and, with a flourish, swept past his frail legs the great bull of fate. His eyes were filled with tears.

Every year on the last evening of the Feria, I meet the same musician at *La Maison Bleue*, he is wearing a brightly-coloured waist-coat and some kind of black head-dress, as he plays with the band from Toulouse's art academy, on some strange kind of small whistle with a string and spinning-top, eyes closed in ecstasy. Every year, at the same moment, in the same place, we greet each other earnestly, wish each other a stimulating year, confident that this ritual shall be repeated over and over again, year after year, because Pierre Arnaud has served us our last shot of the same old eau-de-vie, which invariably tastes of gilded eternity.

Chance is a gentleman one is fortunate enough to come across regularly at Vic. I remember how, one Sunday, at about two in the afternoon, with a hot sun beating down, I walked down to the lower district of Vic, as far as the bodega *Les Sept Péchés Capiteux*. There I met my old friend, Fernand Cousteaux, who is our Pic de la Mirandole for the south-west. A gastronomic columnist at our region's daily, *La Dépêche du Midi*, Fernand is one of those people who can talk endlessly and knowledgeably about the pastel culture at Villefranche-du-Lauragais in the 16th century, go over the arcane details of a Welsh rugby player's style, or launch in poetic and mouth-watering rapture on the art of cooking scallops that have been caught in some other-worldly creek. Economic topics are another subject that fascinates Fernand, who moves around just as easily in the world of bullfighting, which he discusses with the same homeliness as a gardener tends his kitchen-garden. In other words, Fernand is like some oversized library, a library over which hangs the headiness of Armagnac, where books jostle as chaotically as stones on a smuggler's mountain track. That day, he was sitting with Roger Blanchon, a cartoonist, and his wife, in front of a bottle of champagne. They invited me to join them and, together, we set off on the byways of rugby talk. At about five, we pulled our-selves together, almost missing the afternoon corrida, where the bulls seemed to hover, suspended in a world of delicate bubbly.

Vic has a way of greeting visitors that is an art in itself, played out each year with the same operatic crescendo as it welcomes its visitors anew. Saturday kicks off in the arena and downtown like a hesitant score, light music before the fiesta feverishness. Eyes are misty, talk is sluggish, leisurely, as one stands outside the bodegas. Come back the next day and you are plunged in a different world; the tempo now is the invariable tempo of *paseo* music, which is so typical of Vic, a Sevillan mixture of swirling skirts and lowering death. Night falls over the streets of Vic, the *tariquet* has a golden, mellow flavour, one is simply happy to be there, enjoying the simple, untrammelled joys of life. The night air is filled with the fragrance of freedom, and seems to have shaken off the yoke of convention; young women are bare-shouldered, souls are fringed with little red scarves; the city's bourgeois have pulled off their ties and tossed them into the grey inkstand of drab routine.

The bullfighter's suit of lights: a protective armour cloaked in glamour *(opposite)*.

Monday is the third and last act of the Vic opera, marked by mixed flavours of perfection and regrets. Even so, there are very special moments. At *La Maison bleue*, the Brazilian drums finally hit on the right tempo, beat out the warm, balanced rhythm of our multicultural region. At the day's end, everyone is exhausted, but the tune is right. Then, for the last time, bullfighters and their *cuadrillas* leave the ring. Suddenly, it is cool under the conker trees that line the square, but emotions are so intense that time seems suspended. Surely, the Feria must go on… And it does. Year after year. One day, our children will come here, in our steps, remembering us, during the Feria, that window open on a simple, joyful, red-and-gold timelessness. ■

Bullfighting has always had enthusiastic fans in Midi-Pyrénées. In Toulouse, there were no less than eight bullrings during the first half of the 20th century. The biggest and most famous was the Soleil d'Or, which could seat 12,000 spectators; the world's leading bullfighters performed there; but when the owner, Marcel Dangou, died in 1977, there was no-one to take over and the bullfighting tradition was rapidly eroded. Aficionados now gather in Gascony, at Vic-Fezensac, the biggest bullfighting centre in the region, and at Aignan and Gimont. There is talk of bullfighting being reintroduced in Haute-Garonne, at Rieumes and, who knows, Toulouse…

CONTENTS

Printed in October 2001
Imprimeries Fournié - Fonsegrives - Toulouse - France
N° 3089